S-Visa for Material Witnesses

Getting a Work Permit and Legal Status by Being a Material Witness

Attorney Brian D. Lerner

BDL LAW OFFICES OF
BRIAN D. LERNER
A PROFESSIONAL CORPORATION

ATTORNEY DRAFTED IMMIGRATION PETITIONS

By

Brian D. Lerner

Attorney at Law

Disclaimer and Terms of Use:

INTRODUCTION

There are a multitude of different immigration petitions and applications. They are complex and full of requirements. Obviously, it would be best to hire an immigration attorney to best prepare the petitions and applications. However, this can certainly cost thousands of dollars.

The next best option is to get a sample of the petition written by an experienced immigration attorney. The samples cost a fraction what would be charged by an immigration attorney. However, while the reader has to alter, amend and change the parts of the sample petition to reflect their actual situation, it is a fantastic roadmap for them to use. If the reader has purchased the entire petition or application, they will have real live samples of cover letters, forms, declarations, affidavits and the necessary exhibits to use. The samples come from real cases and the names of those clients have been redacted to protect the privacy of that person or corporation.

These are petitions and applications that have been drafted by an experienced immigration attorney with over 25 years of experience. Get the benefits of that experience without the costs.

CONTENTS

About the Law Offices of Brian D. Lerner

Brian D. Lerner has been a licensed attorney since 1992 and started the Law Offices of Brian D. Lerner, APC. The law practice consists of Immigration and Nationality Law and everything involved with and regarding immigration which includes citizenship, investment visas, family and employment visas, removal and deportation hearings, appeals, waivers, adjustment, consulate processing and all types of immigration and citizenship matters. Thousands of families have been reunited and/or permitted to stay in the U.S. and/or return to the U.S. because of the successful work of Immigration Attorney Brian D. Lerner.

This law offices handles all types of immigration cases including family based and employment based. Immigration issues range from immigration court proceedings to trying to fix what paralegals may have done that was neither correct nor proper. Foreign nationals must have experience lawyers admitted to practice law.

The Law Offices of Brian D. Lerner, APC, handles cases arising from business visas, work permits, Green Cards, non-immigrant visas, deportation, citizenship, appeals and all areas of immigration. The Law Offices of Brian D. Lerner, APC does EB-5 Investor Visas, H-1B Specialty Occupation, L-1 Intracompany Transferee, E-2 Treaty Investor, E-1 Treaty Trader, O-1 Extraordinary Ability among others. Regarding immigrant visas for the Green Card, the firm does PERM and advanced degree PERM, Family Petitions, and Extraordinary Alien Petitions. In addition to affirmative petitions, the Law Firm represents people in people in deportation and removal hearings, including political asylum, withholding of removal, and convention against torture cases.

Brian D. Lerner has been certified as an expert in Immigration & Nationality Law by the California State Bar, Board of Legal Specialization since 2000 and has been re-certified three times. He now passes on his decades of experience by allowing the Reader, Law Schools, Professors and other Immigration Attorneys to purchase sample petitions on every facet of Immigration Law.

About the S Nonimmigrant Visa

The S Nonimmigrant Visa allows Foreign Nationals with critical information on criminal or terrorist organizations to come to the U.S. to provide this critical information to law enforcement. There are also different classifications of the S Visa: The S-5 applies to Criminal Informants, the S-6 applies to Terrorist Informants, and the S-7 applies to Accompanying Family members.

LAW OFFICES OF

BRIAN D. LERNER
A PROFESSIONAL CORPORATION

BRIAN D. LERNER, ESQ.
CERTIFIED SPECIALIST IN IMMIGRATION AND NATIONALITY LAW

WWW.CALIFORNIAIMMIGRATION.US

ADMITTED TO THE UNITED STATES SUPREME COURT
ADMITTED TO THE U.S. COURTS OF APPEALS FOR THE 1ST THROUGH 11TH CIRCUITS

3233 EAST BROADWAY · LONG BEACH, CALIFORNIA 90803 · TELEPHONE (562) 495-0554 · FACSIMILE (562) 608-9872

August 14, 2012

████████████████

Office of the U.S. Attorney
312 North Spring Street, 12th Floor
Los Angeles, CA 90012

Re: ███████████████████
     USA v. ███████████████
     12-CR-00218-GW

Dear ██████████:

███████████ (hereinafter "████████"), through undersigned counsel, respectfully requests that your office recommend his case for S visa nonimmigrant classification:

We hereby submit the following documents in support of ██████████ request:

Form   **Description:**

G-28   Notice of Entry of Appearance as Attorney of Representative;
G-325A   Biographic Information; and
I-854   Inter-Agency Alien Witness and Informant Record.

Exhibit: **Description:**

1.   ██████████ Birth Certificate;
2.   ██████████ Marriage Certificate;
3.   ██████████ Spouse's Permanent Resident Card; Fijian Passport; and Oregon
      Instruction Permit;
4.   ██████████ Children's Birth Certificates;
5.   Criminal Docket – 12-CR-00218-GW;
6.   Temporary Identification Letter; and
7.   U.S. Department of State 2011 Reports on Human Rights Practices: Mexico.

I.
SUMMARY OF FACTS

███████ is a 33-year-old male, native and citizen of Mexico. Exhibit 1. ███████ is married to Rajnita W. Prasad, a lawful permanent resident of the United States. Exhibits 2-3. Mr. Herrera and his spouse have 2 U.S. citizen children together, 4-year-old Alondra and 6-year-old Ayesha. Exhibit 4.

███████ first entered the United States in 1999. In October 2010, ███████ returned to Mexico to visit his ailing father. ███████ subsequent attempts to return to the United States were unsuccessful. On February 23, 2012, ███████ along with 18 other individuals, were apprehended by U.S. Customs and Border Protection off the coast of Southern California. ███████ was subsequently released and presumably paroled into the United States as a material witness against the three alien smugglers in his case. Exhibits 5-6. With the assistance of ███████ and other material witnesses, the U.S. Attorney's Office was able to successfully prosecute all three alien smugglers. Exhibit 6.

II.
THE S VISA

S nonimmigrant classification is available to any alien "who the Attorney General determines is in possession of critical reliable information concerning a criminal organization or enterprise, is willing to supply or has supplied such information to Federal or State law enforcement authorities or a Federal or State court, and whose presence in the United States the Attorney General determines is essential to the success of an authorized criminal investigation or the successful prosecution of an individual involved in the criminal organization or enterprise." INA § 101(a)(15)(S)

If the Attorney General considers it to be appropriate, S nonimmigrant classification is also available for "the spouse, married and unmarried sons and daughter, and parents of an alien described in clause (I) . . . if accompanying, or following to join, the alien." INA § 101(a)(15)(S).

The procedure for commencing S nonimmigrant classification is as follows:

1. "Upon the application of a federal or state law enforcement authority ("LEA") . . . pursuant to the filing of Form I-854, Inter-Agency Witness and Informant Record, for nonimmigrant classification described in section 101(a)(15)(S) of the Act, the Commissioner shall determine whether a ground of exclusion exists with respect to the alien for whom classification is sought and, if so, whether it is in the national interest to exercise the discretion to waive the ground of excludability." 8 C.F.R. 212.4(i)(1). Form I-854 "may be used only by a Federal or State and Local LEA." Form I-854, Instructions (05/13/10) at 1. "The certifications made by the alien and . . . the LEA requestor, provide a critical record for the future." Id.

2. Requests for S nonimmigrant classification are submitted to the U.S. Department of Justice. Id. The Department of Justice "shall forward to the Commissioner only qualified applications for S-5 nonimmigrant classification that have been certified in accordance with the provisions of this paragraph and that fall within the annual numerical limitation." 8 C.F.R. 214.2(t)(4)(ii)(C)(1). "The number of aliens who may be provided a visa as nonimmigrants under section 101(a)(15)(S)(i) in any fiscal year may not exceed 200." INA §214(k). The annual numerical limitation "does not include family members." 60 FR 44260 at 44261.

III.
MR. HERRERA'S CASE SHOULD BE RECOMMENDED FOR S VISA NONIMMIGRANT CLASSIFICATION.

1. ███████████ is in possession of critical and reliable information concerning his alien smugglers

███████████ is in possession of critical reliable information concerning his alien smugglers and successful prosecution was possible thanks to the significant information possessed and provided by ██████

2. ███████████ is willing to supply and has supplied critical reliable information to authorities.

███████████ is willing to supply and has supplied critical reliable information to the U.S. Attorney's Office and other law enforcement agencies. With that information the U.S. Attorney's Office was able to secure convictions against all three alien smugglers in USA v. Magallanes-Arias, et al. Although Mr. Herrera was prepared to testify, his testimony was unnecessary as all three alien smugglers pled guilty on July 7, 2012. Exhibit 5.

3. ███████████ was considered essential to the success of an authorized criminal investigation and successful prosecution of individuals involved alien smuggling.

Because ██████ was granted status as a material witness, it is clear that he was useful and essential to the persecution and to the halting of the criminal activities of the three alien smugglers in USA v. Magallanes-Arias, et al. Further, the fact that an investigation and prosecution were successfully concluded does not diminish the contributions that Mr. Herrera made to law enforcement, but instead should be evidence of it.

4. S nonimmigrant classification for ██████ would likely be within the annual numerical limitations set by Congress.

Congress has limited the number of S visas granted per year to 200. INA §214(k). However, this annual numerical limitation "does not include family members." 60 FR 44260 at 44261.

In addition, a Congressional Research Service Report prepared for members and committees of Congress indicates that from 1995 to 2004, only 511 aliens were admitted under the S visa category as opposed to the 2000 that were allowed by Congress.[1] The highest number of S visas granted in one

---

[1] U.S. Congressional Research Service, Immigration: S Visas for Criminal and Terrorist Informants (RS21043; Jan. 23, 2007), by Karma Ester.

Fiscal Year	Informants Admitted	Family Members Admitted
1995	59	77
1996	98	21
1997	35	19
1998	90	56
1999	50	33
2000	21	17
2001	56	22
2002	42	37

year was 98, still less than half of the maximum number allowed by Congress. *Id.* Thus, S nonimmigrant classification for ████████ would likely be within the annual numerical limitations set by Congress.

5. **LEA certification is not an automatic grant of the S nonimmigrant classification, but it is the only gateway through which S nonimmigrant classification can be sought.**

As discussed above, the procedure for commencing S nonimmigrant classification is as follows. First, "upon the application of a federal or state law enforcement authority ("LEA") . . . pursuant to the filing of form I-854, Inter-Agency Witness and Informant Record, for nonimmigrant classification described in section 101(a)(15)(S) of the Act, the Commissioner shall determine whether a ground of exclusion exists with respect to the alien for whom classification is sought and, if so, whether it is in the national interest to exercise the discretion to waive the ground of excludability." 8 C.F.R. 212.4(i)(1). Form I-854 "may be used only by a Federal or State and Local LEA." Form I-854, Instructions (03/31/07), at 1. Therefore, an alien may only apply for S nonimmigrant classification through the Federal LEA to whom he has provided assistance, and this entity in the case of ████████ is the Office of the U.S. Attorney.

Second, requests for S nonimmigrant classification are submitted to the U.S. Department of Justice. *Id.* The Department of Justice "shall forward to the Commissioner only qualified applications for S-5 nonimmigrant classification that have been certified in accordance with the provisions of this paragraph and that fall within the annual numerical limitation." 8 C.F.R. 214.2(t)(4)(ii)(C)(1). Thus, the application proceeds after certification by the LEA, to the Department of Justice who must again approve the application according to its own review of the alien's file, before the alien becomes eligible for the S nonimmigrant classification.

Therefore, S nonimmigrant classification can be initiated only by an LEA. Unless the Office of the U.S. Attorney agrees to initiate the S nonimmigrant classification process for ████████ who has risked his life in order to cooperate with and assist the Office of the U.S. Attorney, ████████ has no chance whatsoever of escaping the dangerous position he may find himself in. Keep in mind that LEA certification is not sufficient in itself because certification by the LEA is only one step towards classification as an S-5 nonimmigrant. If there should be any doubt as to the merits of ████████ request, the multiple levels of review will certainly clarify things. However, given the developments in this relatively new process, specifically *Matter of Garcia-Hernandez*, 23 I&N Dec. 590 (BIA 2003), ████████ only asks that he have a chance to get his case before the Commissioner.

6. ████████ **will likely be harmed or killed should he be forced to return to Mexico.**

In the United States, ████████ is able to benefit from the protection of law enforcement authorities. In Mexico, on the other hand, ████████ would not protected as he cannot rely on Mexican law enforcement to protect himself or his family. Exhibit 7. In fact, as detailed in the U.S. Department of State 2011 Country Reports on Human Right Practice, serious human rights rights issues exist in Mexico including frequent clashes between security forces and Transnational Criminal Organizations (TCOs), kidnappings, arbitrary arrest and detention, corruption and impunity for human rights abuses. Id. Therefore, the dangers that face Mr. Herrera and his family in Mexico are of a completely different nature than the ones that he would face in the United States.

2003	30	28
2004	39	22
Total	511	332

In addition, if ██████████ were sent back to Mexico after his role as an informant to American authorities, he faces grave dangers not only from the associates of the criminal organization but other Mexicans who may resent his "turncoat" behavior. ██████████ would be especially vulnerable because guerrilla or criminal elements may believe that there is some special value in kidnapping someone who has been so valuable to the United States. They may also believe that due to ██████ ██████, assistance that he or his family was rewarded in some way and that this could translate into wealth for the kidnappers. Or they might just want to set an example of Mr. Herrera who betrayed his fellow countrymen.

IV.
CONCLUSION

We understand that your very first priority is criminal prosecution however, we ask that you take some time out of your day to review the enclosed materials and recommend ██████████ case for S visa nonimmigrant classification. ██████████ put his safety at risk in order to aid your office in providing valuable and corroborated information which led to the conviction of three alien smugglers.

Please remember that your recommendation would not be an automatic grant of S visa immigrant classification, but it is essential in order for ██████████ to even be considered for a grant. If you should have any questions, please feel free to contact our office at (562) 495-0554.

Sincerely,

Brian D. Lerner
Attorney at Law

BL:CR: 3616

FORMS

OMB No. 1615-0105; Expires 04/30/2012

G-28, Notice of Entry of Appearance as Attorney or Accredited Representative

Department of Homeland Security

Part 1. Notice of Appearance as Attorney or Accredited Representative

A. This appearance is in regard to Immigration matters before:

☒ USCIS - List the form number(s): I-854

☐ ICE - List the specific matter in which appearance is entered:

☐ CBP - List the specific matter in which appearance is entered:

B. I hereby enter my appearance as attorney or accredited representative at the request of:

List Petitioner, Applicant, or Respondent. NOTE: Provide the mailing address of Petitioner, Applicant, or Respondent being represented, and not the address of the attorney or accredited representative, except when filed under VAWA.

Principal Petitioner, Applicant, or Respondent			A Number or Receipt Number, if any	
Name: Last	First	Middle		☐ Petitioner
				☒ Applicant
		08/08/12	N/A	☐ Respondent
Address: Street Number and Street Name		Apt. No. City	State Zip Code	

Pursuant to the Privacy Act of 1974 and DHS policy, I hereby consent to the disclosure to the named Attorney or Accredited Representative of any record pertaining to me that appears in any system of records of USCIS, USCBP, or USICE.

Signature of Petitioner, Applicant, or Respondent   Date

Part 2. Information about Attorney or Accredited Representative *(Check applicable items(s) below)*

A. ☒ I am an attorney and a member in good standing of the bar of the highest court(s) of the following State(s), possession(s), territory(ies), commonwealth(s), or the District of Columbia: **Supreme Court of California**

I am not ☒ or ☐ am subject to any order of any court or administrative agency disbarring, suspending, enjoining, restraining, or otherwise restricting me in the practice of law (If you are subject to any order(s), explain fully on reverse side).

B. ☐ I am an accredited representative of the following qualified non-profit religious, charitable, social service, or similar organization established in the United States, so recognized by the Department of Justice, Board of Immigration Appeals pursuant to 8 CFR 1292.2. Provide name of organization and expiration date of accreditation:

C. ☐ I am associated with _____

The attorney or accredited representative of record previously filed Form G-28 in this case, and my appearance as an attorney or accredited representative is at his or her request. (If you check this item, also complete item A or B above in Part 2, whichever is appropriate).

Part 3. Name and Signature of Attorney or Accredited Representative

I have read and understand the regulations and conditions contained in 8 CFR 103.2 and 292 governing appearances and representation before the Department of Homeland Security. I declare under penalty of perjury under the laws of the United States that the information I have provided on this form is true and correct.

Name of Attorney or Accredited Representative	Attorney Bar Number(s), if any
Brian D. Lerner	158536
Signature of Attorney or Accredited Representative	Date

Complete Address of Attorney or Organization of Accredited Representative (Street Number and Street Name, Suite No., City, State, Zip Code)

Law Offices of Brian D. Lerner, APC 3233 E. Broadway Long Beach, CA 90803

Phone Number *(Include area code)*	Fax Number, if any *(Include area code)*	E-Mail Address, if any
(562) 495-0554	(562) 608-8672	blerner@californiaimmigration.us

Form G-28 (Rev. 04/22/09)N

OMB No. 1615-0008; Expires 08/31/2012

Department of Homeland Security
U.S. Citizenship and Immigration Services

G-325A, Biographic Information

(Family Name)	(First Name)	(Middle Name)	☒ Male ☐ Female	Date of Birth (mm/dd/yyyy) 03/06/1979	Citizenship/Nationality Mexican	File Number A N/A

All Other Names Used (include names by previous marriages)	City and Country of Birth	U.S. Social Security # (if any) N/A

	Family Name	First Name	Date of Birth (mm/dd/yyyy)	City, and Country of Birth (if known)	City and Country of Residence
Father			04/05/1945	Cerrital de Gelaena Mexico	Deceased
Mother (Maiden Name)			09/17/1950	San Juan las Huertas Mexico	San Juan Las Huertas Mexico

Current Husband or Wife (If none, so state) Family Name (For wife, give maiden name)	First Name	Date of Birth (mm/dd/yyyy)	City and Country of Birth	Date of Marriage	Place of Marriage
Wife		05/07/2084	Nausori Fiji	03/01/2009	Beaverton, OR

Former Husbands or Wives (If none, so state) First Name Family Name (For wife, give maiden name)		Date of Birth (mm/dd/yyyy)	Date and Place of Marriage	Date and Place of Termination of Marriage
None				

Applicant's residence last five years. List present address first.

Street and Number	City	Province or State	Country	From Month	From Year	To Month	To Year
	Beaverton	OR	USA	03	2012	Present Time	
	San Juan las Huertas	Oaxaca	Mexico	10	2010	01	2012
	Beaverton	OR	USA	03	2009	10	2010
	Beaverton	OR	USA	03	2008	03	2009
	Beaverton	OR	USA	03	2007	03	2008

Applicant's last address outside the United States of more than one year.

Street and Number	City	Province or State	Country	From Month	From Year	To Month	To Year
	San Juan las Huertas	Oaxaca	Mexico	10	2010	01	2012

Applicant's employment last five years. (If none, so state.) List present employment first.

Full Name and Address of Employer	Occupation (Specify)	From Month	From Year	To Month	To Year
3745 Southwest 114th Avenue #11 Beaverton, OR 97005	Manager/ Supervisor			Present Time	

Last occupation abroad if not shown above. (Include all information requested above.)

None

This form is submitted in connection with an application for: ☐ Naturalization ☒ Other (Specify): S-Visa ☐ Status as Permanent Resident	Signature of Applicant	Date 8/08/12

If your native alphabet is in other than Roman letters, write your name in your native alphabet below:

Penalties: Severe penalties are provided by law for knowingly and willfully falsifying or concealing a material fact.

Applicant: Print your name and Alien Registration Number in the box outlined by heavy border below.

Complete This Box (Family Name)	(Given Name)	(Middle Name)	(Alien Registration Number) A N/A

Form G-325A (Rev. 08/08/11) Y

3616

OMB No. 1615-0046, Expires 05/31/2013

Department of Homeland Security
U.S. Citizenship and Immigration Services

Form I-854, Inter-Agency Alien Witness and Informant Record

Part A. To be completed by Law Enforcement Agencies *(See instructions for specific information.)*
Information must be Typed or Printed clearly.

1. Name of LEA/Requestor: _____

2. Requesting Agent: _____ Control Agent: _____

   Address: _____ Phone No.*(Including Area Code)*: _____

   _____ Fax No.*(Including Area Code)*: _____

Check if applicable:

3. ☒ Alien will be placed in danger in ☐ U.S. ☒ abroad as a result of providing information, etc.

   ☒ Alien poses no danger to people or property of the U.S.

   ☐ If the alien poses a danger, the danger posed by the alien is outweighed by the assistance the alien will furnish.

   ☒ Investigation. ☒ Prosecution. ☐ United States Attorney involvement.

4. Type of Request(s). *(Attach legal basis for request.)*

   ☒ S-5 ☐ S-6

   Consular post at which visa will be sought: _____

   ☐ Change of Status - If change of status is requested, current immigration status is _____

   ☒ Adjustment of Status *(Go to Part F after completing information in items 5, 6 and 7 below.)*

   ☐ Fees attached *(when applicable)* ☐ Security concerns, State special instructions regarding security precautions.

NOTE: Provide a clear statement of the operations that form the basis of the request (e.g., Grand Jury subpoena), the objective of the request and any bargain the requestor wishes to make or has made with the alien. Attach a complete criminal history, FBI No. and U.S. Social Security Number.

5. Alien's Name *(Last Name, First and Middle)*		Other Names Used	
███████████████		███████████	
Alien's Address *(Street Number and Name)*		A #	I-94 #
████████████████████		N/A	N/A
City	State or Province	Zip/Postal Code	Current Location of Alien
Beaverton	OR	97005	OR
Marital Status	Date of Birth (mm/dd/yyyy)	Place of Birth *(City or Country)*	Citizenship/Nationality	Occupation
Married	03/06/1979	Mexico	Mexico	Janitor
Date of Last Entry into U.S. (mm/dd/yyyy): 02/23/2012		☒ Form G-325 attached	☐ Form FD-258 attached	☐ Photos attached

6. On a separate application, provide all information requested in **item 5** above for each beneficiary who seeks derivative status - spouse, parents and all sons and daughters of the alien for whom an S classification is requested. *(Attach additional sheets of paper as necessary.)*

Form I-854 (Rev. 05/13/10)Y

7a. The following information must be provided for each alien named in items 5 and 6 above.

Has the alien, while outside of the United States, ever committed, ordered, incited, assisted, or otherwise participated in genocide, torture, or extrajudicial killing or participated in Nazi persecution?

☐ Yes   ☒ No   *If yes please write a detailed statement below and attach any relevant documents. (Attach additional sheets of paper as needed.)*

_____

_____

_____

_____

_____

_____

_____

_____

7b. For the above named alien, I request waiver(s) of the following grounds of inadmissibility. *(Check all possible grounds and attach all relevant documents establishing the grounds of inadmissibility and why you feel a waiver is appropriate for this alien. This information must be provided for each alien named in items 5 and 6 above. Copy this check list of the grounds of inadmissibility for each derivative.)*

☐ Communicable disease	☐ Controlled substance trafficker
☐ Immigrant visa issued outside numerical limitation	☐ Prostitute and/or Procurer of Prostitution
☐ Crime involving moral turpitude	☐ Exercised diplomatic immunity to avoid prosecution
☐ International child abduction	☐ Unlawful activity related to National Security
☐ Multiple criminal convictions	☐ Terrorist activities
☐ Engaged in unlawful commercialized vice	☐ Communist Party member
☐ Entrance prejudicial to public	☐ Public charge
☐ Involved in espionage, sabotage or laws relating to technology	☐ Lacking labor certification
☐ Coming to overthrow the U.S. Government	☐ Fraud/Misrepresentation
☐ Foreign policy exclusion	☐ Immigrant without a visa
☐ Unqualified physician	☐ Draft evader-was immigrant when left U.S.
☐ Previously removed - aggravated felony	☐ Alien accompanying helpless inadmissible alien
☐ Stowaway	☐ Violator of section 274C
☐ Nonimmigrant without a valid passport or visa	☐ Ordered, incited, assisted or otherwise participated in the commission of the acts of torture or extra judicial killing
☐ Previously excluded and deported or removed	☐ Engaged in conduct relating to severe violations of religious freedoms
☐ Alien smuggler	
☐ Physical/mental disorder (dangerous)	☐ Weapons charges, domestic violence, and money laundering
☐ Drug abuser or addict	☐ Other
☐ Convicted of law pertaining to controlled substances	☒ No waivers are requested/needed

Part B. Certifications

1. Alien Certification *(S classification request)*

I certify under penalty of perjury that I have reviewed with the LEA all the information in **Part A**, disclosed all information to the best of my ability, and disclosed all reasons for which I may be removed from the United States; that I shall report at least every three months my whereabouts and activities as the above LEA shall require; that I understand I am subject to removal for any grounds of inadmissibility (conduct or condition) not disclosed at this time or for conduct committed after admission to the United States; that I shall abide by all conditions, limitations and restrictions imposed upon my entry; that the classification I seek is temporary and will terminate within three (3) years; that I am restricted by the terms of my admission to very specific means by which I will be able to remain permanently in the United States; that I will pay Social Security and all applicable taxes on all employment in the United States; and that I hereby waive my right to a removal hearing and to contest, other than on the basis of an application for withholding of removal, any action for deportation instituted against me.

Certification: I certify that I have read and understand all the questions and statements on this form. If I do not understand English, I further acknowledge that this has been read to me in a language I do understand. The answers I have furnished are true and correct to the best of my knowledge and belief.

Signature	Date *(mm dd yyyy)*

LEA Witness	Title	Date *(mm dd yyyy)*

Translator	Language Used	Date *(mm dd yyyy)*

2. LEA Certification

I certify the above information is true and correct to the best of my knowledge; that I may make, have made, and will make no promises regarding the above alien's ability to adjust status or stay permanently in the United States other than those that comport with section 101(a)(15)(S) of the Act; that I will collect quarterly reports detailing the above alien's whereabouts and activities and forward required information to the Criminal Division; that I will immediately report to U.S. Immigration and Customs Enforcement, DHS if this alien fails to report quarterly or fails to comply or to cooperate with the terms and conditions of admission or if the alien commits any removable activity after the date of admission. I further certify that I assume complete law enforcement responsibility for control and continued stay in lawful status of the alien, including necessary monitoring, travel arrangements for arrival and departure, safety precautions and specified conditions of stay or departure; that I have provided a sworn declaration as to the basis of this application and checked all available database information on the above alien, and that I have carefully reviewed the above statements with the alien to ensure that all terms and conditions are understood.

☐ Translation *(This serves to verify the alien's certification of translation. See Page 2, Part B.1. of this form.)*

Signature of HQ Chief of LEA	Title of Certifier	Date *(mm dd yyyy)*

Name of Agency Contact	Phone No. *(Including Area Code)*

Form I-854 (Rev. 03/13/19)Y Page 3

3. For United States Attorney Use Only *(if applicable)*

Because the alien's presence is essential to the success of a Federal or State investigation or prosecution, the United States Attorney recommends the above request be granted and further certifies that there has not been and will not be any promises at all regarding the above alien's ability to adjust status or stay permanently in the United States, other than those that comport with section 101(a)(15)(S) of the Act.

_____   _____
Signature   Date *(mm dd yyyy)*

_____   _____
Office   Phone No.*(Including Area Code)*

4. For U.S. Department of State/Rewards Committee - S6 Classification use only

After checking all information, the U.S. Department of State:

☐ Certifies the alien is eligible to receive an award under 22 U.S.C 2708(a).

☐ Certifies the alien is not eligible for such award.   Date *(mm dd yyyy)*

_____   _____   _____
Signature   Date *(mm dd yyyy)*   Phone No.*(Including Area Code)*

_____   _____
Title   Office

Part C. For Department of Justice, Criminal Division Use Only

After checking and evaluating all waiver and other information available, the Department of Homeland Security, U.S. Immigration and Customs Enforcement and Department of Justice, Criminal Division:

☐ Certify that, pursuant to section 101(a)(15)(S) of the Act and the request of the above LEA, the above alien is recommended for the S classification requested, that the above request(s) for waivers of inadmissibility appear to warrant approval, that all conditions and limitations of the request for classification are attached, that this request falls within the numerical limitation for an S visa and that, therefore, this request is forwarded to the Assistant Secretary of Immigration and Customs Enforcement for approval.

☐ Deny request

_____   _____   _____
Signature   Date *(mm dd yyyy)*   Phone No.*(Including Area Code)*

_____   _____
Title   Office

Form I-854 (Rev. 05 13 10)Y Page 4

Part D. For U.S. Immigration and Customs Enforcement Use Only

☐ Fee Received (If applicable)　☐ Request Denied　☐ Request Granted

☐ Waiver(s) of Grounds of Inadmissibility

Note all grounds waived and conditions attached thereto.

Signature	Date (mm/dd/yyyy)	Phone No.(Including Area Code)

Title	Office

Part E. For U.S. Citizenship and Immigration Services Use Only

LEA Request:　☐ Granted　☐ Forward to DOS/VO　☐ Denied

☐ Change of Classification Granted　☐ Denied

Signature	Date (mm/dd/yyyy)	Phone No.(Including Area Code)

Title	Office

Part F. For Department of State/Visa Office Use Only

☐ Forwarded to Consul by VO for Visa Approval　☐ Not Forwarded

Signature	Date (mm/dd/yyyy)	Phone No.(Including Area Code)

Title	Office

☐ Visa Granted

☐ Visa Denied　　Signature　　　　Date (mm/dd/yyyy)

Title	Office

Form I-854 (Rev. 05/13/10)Y Page 5

Part G. Request to allow an S Nonimmigrant to file for adjustment of status to permanent resident

(For Department of Justice, Criminal Division Use Only)

(Please attach all relevant documentation establishing (1) the information certified below; (2) the recommendations and reasons for the certified recommendations.)

1. Name of LEA: _____ submitting request to allow an S nonimmigrant to file for adjustment of status.

   Date Submitted *(mm dd yyyy)* _____

2. Criminal Division (Assistant Attorney General) Certifications.

   I certify that (alien's name) _____ has -

   If S-5:
   - [ ] Supplied the information that formed the basis of entry;
   - [ ] The information substantially contributed to the success of an authorized criminal investigation or the prosecution of an individual as per terms of entry.

   If S-6:
   - [ ] Supplied the information that formed the basis of entry;
   - [ ] The information substantially contributed to the prevention or frustration of an act of terrorism against a U.S. person or property or the success of an authorized criminal investigation of, or the prosecution of, an individual involved in such an act of terrorism.
   - [ ] Has received a reward under section 36(a) of the State Department Basic Authorities Act of 1956;

   If S-5 or S-6:
   - [ ] Has abided by all the terms, conditions and specific 22 U.S.C. 2708(a) limitations of the S classification.

   Other Comments:

   _____

   _____

   _____

Signature	Date *(mm dd yyyy)*	Phone No. *(Including Area Code)*
Title	Office	

3. For U.S. Citizenship and Immigration Services Use Only

   [ ] Adjustment   [ ] Other Action

Signature	Date *(mm dd yyyy)*	Phone No. *(Including Area Code)*
Title	Office	

Form I-854 (Rev. 05-13-10)Y Page 6

EXHIBITS

ESTADOS UNIDOS MEXICANOS
REGISTRO CIVIL

No. 795786

EN NOMBRE DEL ESTADO LIBRE Y SOBERANO DE OAXACA Y COMO **OFICIAL** DEL REGISTRO CIVIL

CERTIFICO QUE EN EL LIBRO № _____ **DEL** REGISTRO CIVIL QUE ES A MI CARGO

EN LA FOJA № _____ SE ENCUENTRA ASENTADA EL **ACTA №.** _____ DE FECH

LEVANTADA POR **EL C.** OFICIAL _____

DEL REGISTRO CIVIL _____

EN LA CUAL SE CONTIENEN **LOS** SIGUIENTES DATOS

Valor
$ 200.00
(Doscientos Pesos)

ACTA DE NACIMIENTO

NOMBRE _____

FECHA DE NACIMIENTO _____ HORA _____

PRESENTADO: VIVO ○ MUERTO ○ SEXO: MASCULINO ○ FEMENINO ○

LUGAR DE NACIMIENTO _____

COMPARECIO: EL PADRE ○ LA MADRE ○ AMBOS ○ PERSONA DISTINTA ○

PADRES

NOMBRE ▆▆▆▆▆▆▆ NACIONALIDAD _____ EDAD _____

NOMBRE _____ NACIONALIDAD _____ EDAD _____

ABUELOS

ABUELO PATERNO ▆▆▆▆▆▆▆ NACIONALIDAD _____

ABUELA PATERNA _____ NACIONALIDAD _____

ABUELO MATERNO _____ NACIONALIDAD _____

ABUELA MATERNA _____ NACIONALIDAD _____

TESTIGOS

NOMBRE ▆▆▆▆▆ NACIONALIDAD _____ EDAD _____

NOMBRE ▆▆▆▆▆ NACIONALIDAD _____ EDAD _____

CURP _____

PERSONA DISTINTA DE LOS PADRES QUE PRESENTA AL REGISTRADO

NOMBRE _____ PARENTESCO _____ EDAD _____

SE EXTIENDE ESTA CERTIFICACION, EN CUMPLIMIENTO DEL ARTICULO 52 DEL CODIGO

CIVIL VIGENTE EN EL ESTADO EN _____

A LOS _____ DIAS DEL MES DE _____ DE _____

SELLO DE LA OFI
DEL REGISTRO C

EL OFICIAL DEL REGISTRO CIVIL DOY FE

C. LIC. RAFAEL ORTIZ VASQUEZ.

Marriage Certificate

No. 2009-343

This is to certify that the undersigned, a _____ JUDGE _____
(title of person solemnizing marriage)

authority of a license bearing date the _____ 27TH _____ day of FEBRUARY, 2009

issued by the County of WASHINGTON, State of Oregon, did on this _____ 1ST _____

day of _____ MARCH _____, A.D., 2009, at _____

(location)

join in lawful wedlock

▮▮▮▮▮▮▮▮▮▮▮▮▮▮

and _____ RuBrand. _____

with their mutual consent and in the presence of the witnesses undersigned below

Signature of Groom: _____

Name: _____

Address: _____

Signature of Bride: _____

Name: _____

Address: _____

Witness: _____

Name: _____

Address: _____

Name/Address of person solemnizing religious

Name: _____

Address: _____

Name/Address of person authorizing religious

Roger Deal

Name of County Official Issuing License

Witness: _____

Name: _____

Address: _____

This is a souvenir certificate. This certificate should not be used in place of a legal marriage record.

REPUBLIC OF THE
FIJI ISLANDS
PASSPORT

REPUBLIC OF THE FIJI ISLANDS

PASSPORT
PASSEPORT

P   FJI

CITIZEN OF THE REPUBLIC OF THE FIJI ISLANDS

07 MAY 1984   NAUSORI, FIJI

F   IMMIGRATION DEPARTMENT

02 SEP 2003

02 SEP 2013   RNRapp

<<<<<<<<<<<<<<<<<<

602390<<<2FJI8405070F1309021<<<<<<<<<<<<<<<04

PERMANENT RESIDENT CARD

IUSA0558303636LIN0815650472<<
I405070F1805051FJI<<<<<<<<<<<5

OREGON

7328550

OREGON DEPARTMENT OF HUMAN SERVICES
HEALTH DIVISION
Center For Health Statistics   136-
CERTIFICATE OF LIVE BIRTH

002256

Type or print in
permanent black ink
See handbook for
instructions

CHILD

CHILD - NAME   First   Middle   Last   SEX   DATE OF BIRTH
                                                        Female   1a. March 23, 2006

TIME OF BIRTH   FACILITY - NAME (if not in hospital, or clinic, give address)   CITY, TOWN, OR LOCATION OF BIRTH   COUNTY OF BIRTH
2a. 1939   5a. Emanuel Hospital   4c. Multnomah

CERTIFIER

SIGNATURE   DATE SIGNED   CERTIFIER - NAME AND TITLE
                                    3/26/06   Birth Clerk

NAME AND TITLE OF ATTENDANT AT BIRTH IF OTHER THAN CERTIFIER   ATTENDANT MAILING ADDRESS
Christine Kenlan, C.N.M.

DATE FILED BY LOCAL REG.   REGISTRAR - SIGNATURE
MAR 3 0 2006   Dorthy L. Sampson

MOTHER

MOTHER - NAME   First   Middle   Last   MAIDEN SURNAME   DATE OF BIRTH   STATE OF BIRTH
                                                7b. Prasad   7c. May 07, 1984 7d. Fiji

                CITY   CITY, TOWN, OR LOCATION   STREET AND NUMBER
8c. Oregon   Washington   8c. Beaverton

INSIDE CITY LIMITS   ZIP CODE   MOTHER'S MAILING ADDRESS AND ZIP CODE (if same as Above, leave blank)
8c. Yes   97005-

FATHER

FATHER - NAME   First   Middle   Last   DATE OF BIRTH   STATE OF BIRTH
10a. Jose   Herrera Lopez   10e. Mar 06, 1979 10c. Mexico

INFORMANT

I certify that the personal information provided on this certificate is correct to the best of my knowledge and belief.

11. /s/Rajnita Prasad

THIS IS A TRUE AND EXACT REPRODUCTION OF THE DOCUMENT OFFICIALLY
REGISTERED AT THE OFFICE OF THE MULTNOMAH COUNTY REGISTRAR

APR 0 6 2006

DATE ISSUED

LELA WICKHAM, RN, MS
COUNTY REGISTRAR
MULTNOMAH COUNTY, OREGON

THIS COPY IS NOT VALID WITHOUT RAISED SEAL AND BORDER

OREGON DEPARTMENT OF HUMAN SERVICES
CENTER FOR HEALTH STATISTICS

CERTIFICATE OF LIVE BIRTH

136-2008-043737
STATE FILE NUMBER

CHILD

1. Child's Name (First, Middle Name(s), Last Name(s), Suffix)

2. Sex	3a. Date of Birth	3b. Time of Birth	4a. County of Birth
Female	November 20, 2008	1703	Multnomah

4b. Facility Of Birth	4c. City, Town, or Location of Birth
Legacy	Portland

MOTHER

5a. Current Legal Name	5b. Name Prior to First Marriage

5c. Residence — State	5d. County	5e. City, Town or Location
Oregon	Washington	Beaverton

5f. Street and Number		5g. Zip Code
		97005

5g. Date of Birth	6b. Birthplace
May 07, 1984	Fiji

FATHER

8a. Date of Birth	8b. Birthplace

7. Current Legal Name

INFORMANT

9. Informant's Name and Relationship to Child

CERTIFIER

10b. Name and Title of Attendant at Birth if Other than Certifier

Certified Nurse Midwife

10c. I certify that this child was born alive at the place, time and date stated.	Electronically Signed	10d. Title of Certifier	10e. Date Signed
		Birth Clerk	November 23, 2008

11a. Registrar's Signature	Electronically Signed	11b. Date Filed	Local File Number
		November 23, 2008	

12. Amendment

45-1CC (01/08)

Certificate of Birth

This certifies that

_____

was born to

_____

at Legacy Emanuel Hospital & Health Center
Portland, Oregon

at 5:03 pm on Thursday

the 20th day of November 2008

In witness whereof the said hospital has caused
this certificate to be signed by its duly authorized officer, and
its official seal to be hereunto affixed.

Attending Physician/Certified Nurse Midwife

Birth Nurse

Case title: USA v ███████████ et al   Date Filed: 03/09/2012
Magistrate judge case number: 2:12-mj-00468-DUTY

Assigned to: Judge George H Wu

Defendant (1)

████████████████

Reg # 62396-112

represented by **Michael S Chernis**
Abner Chernis LLP
3110 Main Street Suite 205
Santa Monica, CA 90405
310-566-4388
Fax: 310-382-2541
Email: mchernis@abnerchernis.com
ATTORNEY TO BE NOTICED
Designation: CJA Appointment

Pending Counts

8:1324(a)(1)(A)(v)(I),(a)(1)(A)(i),(a)(1)(B)(i)
CONSPIRACY TO BRING ALIENS TO
THE UNITED STATES
(1)

8:1324(a)(1)(A)(i),(a)(1)(B)(i)BRINGING
ALIENS TO THE UNITED STATES
(2-17)

8:1324(a)(2)(B)(ii) BRINGING ALIENS
TO THE UNITED STATES FOR
PRIVATE FINANCIAL GAIN
(18-21)

8:1324(a)(2)(B)(ii) BRINGING ALIENS
TO THE UNITED STATES FOR
PRIVATE FINANCIAL GAIN
(22)

8:1324(a)(2)(B)(ii) BRINGING ALIENS
TO THE UNITED STATES FOR
PRIVATE FINANCIAL GAIN
(23-33)

Disposition

Highest Offense Level (Opening)

Felony

Terminated Counts	Disposition
None	

Highest Offense Level (Terminated)

None

Complaints	Disposition
Defendants in violation of 8:1324(a)(1)(A)(v)(I)	

Assigned to: Judge George H Wu

Defendant (2)

████████████████████████

Reg # 62395-112

represented by **Paul E Potter**
Potter & Cohen
3852 East Colorado Boulevard
Pasadena, CA 91107-3989
626-795-0681
Email: ppotter@pottercohenlaw.com
ATTORNEY TO BE NOTICED
Designation: CJA Appointment

Pending Counts

8:1324(a)(1)(A)(v)(I),(a)(1)(A)(i),(a)(1)(B)(i)
CONSPIRACY TO BRING ALIENS TO
THE UNITED STATES
(1)

8:1324(a)(1)(A)(i),(a)(1)(B)(i)BRINGING
ALIENS TO THE UNITED STATES
(2-17)

8:1324(a)(2)(B)(ii) BRINGING ALIENS
TO THE UNITED STATES FOR
PRIVATE FINANCIAL GAIN
(18-20)

8:1324(a)(2)(B)(ii) BRINGING ALIENS
TO THE UNITED STATES FOR
PRIVATE FINANCIAL GAIN
(21)

8:1324(a)(2)(B)(ii) BRINGING ALIENS
TO THE UNITED STATES FOR
PRIVATE FINANCIAL GAIN
(22-33)

Disposition

<u>Highest Offense Level (Opening)</u>

Felony

<u>Terminated Counts</u>   Disposition

None

<u>Highest Offense Level (Terminated)</u>

None

<u>Complaints</u>   Disposition

Defendants in violation of
8:1324(a)(1)(A)(v)(I)

Assigned to: Judge George H Wu

<u>Defendant (3)</u>

▮▮▮▮▮▮▮▮▮▮   represented by **Richard P Lasting**
                                                  Richard P Lasting Law Offices
Reg # 22978-298   315 East 8th Street, Suite 801
                                                  Los Angeles, CA 90014
                                                  213-489-9025
                                                  Fax: 310-626-9677
                                                  Email: richardplasting@sbcglobal.net
                                                  ATTORNEY TO BE NOTICED
                                                  Designation: CJA Appointment

<u>Pending Counts</u>   Disposition

8:1324(a)(1)(A(v)(I),(a)(1)(A)(i),(a)(1)(B)(i)
CONSPIRACY TO BRING ALIENS TO
THE UNITED STATES
(1)

8:1324(a)(1)(A)(i),(a)(1)(B)(i)BRINGING
ALIENS TO THE UNITED STATES
(2-17)

8:1324(a)(2)(B)(ii) BRINGING ALIENS
TO THE UNITED STATES FOR
PRIVATE FINANCIAL GAIN
(18-20)

8:1324(a)(2)(B)(ii) BRINGING ALIENS
TO THE UNITED STATES FOR
PRIVATE FINANCIAL GAIN
(21)

8:1324(a)(2)(B)(ii) BRINGING ALIENS
TO THE UNITED STATES FOR

PRIVATE FINANCIAL GAIN
(22-33)

Highest Offense Level (Opening)

Felony

Terminated Counts   Disposition

None

Highest Offense Level (Terminated)

None

Complaints   Disposition

Defendants in violation of
8:1324(a)(1)(A)(v)(I)

Material Witness

███████████████   represented by Charles C Brown
                                           Federal Public Defenders Office
                                           321 East 2nd Street
                                           Los Angeles, CA 90012-4202
                                           213-894-1700
                                           Fax: 213-894-0081
                                           Email:
                                           zzCAC_FPD_Document_Receiving@fd.org
                                           LEAD ATTORNEY
                                           ATTORNEY TO BE NOTICED
                                           Designation: Public Defender or
                                           Community Defender Appointment

Material Witness

Adolfo Pina-Mejia   represented by Charles C Brown
                                           (See above for address)
                                           LEAD ATTORNEY
                                           ATTORNEY TO BE NOTICED
                                           Designation: Public Defender or
                                           Community Defender Appointment

Material Witness

Francisco Cruz-Mencinas   represented by Charles C Brown
                                           (See above for address)

LEAD ATTORNEY
ATTORNEY TO BE NOTICED
Designation: Public Defender or
Community Defender Appointment

Material Witness

██████████████

represented by **Charles C Brown**
(See above for address)
LEAD ATTORNEY
ATTORNEY TO BE NOTICED
Designation: Public Defender or
Community Defender Appointment

Material Witness

██████████████

represented by **Charles C Brown**
(See above for address)
LEAD ATTORNEY
ATTORNEY TO BE NOTICED
Designation: Public Defender or
Community Defender Appointment

Material Witness

███████████████

represented by **Charles C Brown**
(See above for address)
LEAD ATTORNEY
ATTORNEY TO BE NOTICED
Designation: Public Defender or
Community Defender Appointment

Federal Public Defender
Federal Public Defenders Office
321 East 2nd Street
Los Angeles, CA 90012-4206
213-894-2854
Email:
zzCAC_FPD_Document_Receiving@fd.org
ATTORNEY TO BE NOTICED
Designation: Public Defender or
Community Defender Appointment

Material Witness

███████████████

represented by **Charles C Brown**

(See above for address)
LEAD ATTORNEY
ATTORNEY TO BE NOTICED
Designation: Public Defender or
Community Defender Appointment

Federal Public Defender
(See above for address)
ATTORNEY TO BE NOTICED
Designation: Public Defender or
Community Defender Appointment

<u>Material Witness</u>

████████████████   represented by   **Charles C Brown**
(See above for address)
LEAD ATTORNEY
ATTORNEY TO BE NOTICED
Designation: Public Defender or
Community Defender Appointment

Federal Public Defender
(See above for address)
ATTORNEY TO BE NOTICED
Designation: Public Defender or
Community Defender Appointment

<u>Material Witness</u>

██████████████████████   represented by   **Charles C Brown**
(See above for address)
LEAD ATTORNEY
ATTORNEY TO BE NOTICED
Designation: Public Defender or
Community Defender Appointment

Federal Public Defender
(See above for address)
ATTORNEY TO BE NOTICED
Designation: Public Defender or
Community Defender Appointment

<u>Material Witness</u>

████████████████   represented by   **Charles C Brown**
(See above for address)
LEAD ATTORNEY

represented by **Charles C Brown**
(See above for address)
LEAD ATTORNEY
ATTORNEY TO BE NOTICED
Designation: Public Defender or
Community Defender Appointment

Federal Public Defender
(See above for address)
ATTORNEY TO BE NOTICED
Designation: Public Defender or
Community Defender Appointment

Plaintiff

USA

represented by **Christina T Shay**
AUSA - Office of US Attorney
312 North Spring Street 12th Floor
Los Angeles, CA 90012
213-894-0757
Fax: 213-894-0141
Email: christina.shay@usdoj.gov
ATTORNEY TO BE NOTICED

Date Filed	#	Docket Text
02/27/2012	1	COMPLAINT filed as to ▮▮▮▮▮▮▮▮▮▮▮▮▮▮▮▮▮▮ Serrano, Juan Ramirez-Layva in violation of 8:1324(a)(1)(A)(v)(I). Approved by Magistrate Judge Charles F. Eick as to . ▮▮▮▮▮▮▮▮▮▮▮▮▮▮▮ ▮▮▮▮▮▮▮▮▮▮▮▮▮▮▮▮▮▮ (3). (ja) [2:12-mj-00468-DUTY] (Entered: 02/29/2012)
02/27/2012	8	REPORT COMMENCING CRIMINAL ACTION as to Defendant Juan Ramirez-Layva; defendant's Year of Birth: 1987; date of arrest: 2/23/2012 (ja) [2:12-mj-00468-DUTY] (Entered: 03/01/2012)
02/27/2012	9	MINUTES OF INITIAL APPEARANCE ON LOCAL COMPLAINT held before Magistrate Judge Charles F. Eick Defendant arraigned and advised of the charges. Defendant states true name as charged.Attorney: Richard P Lasting for Juan Ramirez-Layva, Appointed, present. Court orders defendant permanently detained. Defendant remanded to the custody of the U.S. Marshal. Preliminary Hearing set for 3/12/2012 04:30 PM before Duty Magistrate Judge. Post-Indictment Arraignment set for 3/19/2012 08:30 AM before Duty Magistrate Judge. (SPANISH) INTERPRETER Required Court Smart: CS 2/27/12. (ja) [2:12-mj-00468-DUTY] (Entered: 03/01/2012)
02/27/2012	10	NOTICE OF REQUEST FOR DETENTION filed by Plaintiff USA as to Defendant Juan Ramirez-Layva (ja) [2:12-mj-00468-DUTY] (Entered: 03/01/2012)
02/27/2012	11	ORDER OF DETENTION by Magistrate Judge Charles F. Eick as to Defendant Juan Ramirez-Layva (ja) [2:12-mj-00468-DUTY] (Entered: 03/01/2012)

02/27/2012	12	NOTICE DIRECTING DEFENDANT TO APPEAR for Preliminary Hearing and Arraignment on Indictment/Information. Defendant Juan Ramirez-Layva is directed to appear for Preliminary Hearing on 3/12/12 at 4:30 P.M. and for Post Indictment Arraignment on 3/19/12 at 8:30 A.M. before the Duty Magistrate Judge. (ja) [2:12-mj-00468-DUTY] (Entered: 03/01/2012)
02/27/2012	27	FINANCIAL AFFIDAVIT filed as to Defendant ███████████ (mhe) [2:12-mj-00468-DUTY] (Entered: 03/01/2012)
02/27/2012	13	REPORT COMMENCING CRIMINAL ACTION as to Defendant ███████ ████████ defendant's Year of Birth: 1978; date of arrest: 2/23/2012 (ja) [2:12-mj-00468-DUTY] (Entered: 03/01/2012)
02/27/2012	14	MINUTES OF INITIAL APPEARANCE ON LOCAL COMPLAINT held before Magistrate Judge Charles F. Eick Defendant arraigned and advised of the charges. Defendant states true name as charged. Attorney: Paul E Potter for ██████ ████████████ Appointed, present. Court orders defendant permanently detained. Defendant remanded to the custody of the U.S. Marshal. Preliminary Hearing set for 3/12/2012 04:30 PM before Duty Magistrate Judge., Post-Indictment Arraignment set for 3/19/2012 08:30 AM before Duty Magistrate Judge. (SPANISH) INTERPRETER Required Court Smart: CS 2/27/12. (ja) [2:12-mj-00468-DUTY] (Entered: 03/01/2012)
02/27/2012	15	NOTICE OF REQUEST FOR DETENTION filed by Plaintiff USA as to Defendant ████████████████) (ja) [2:12-mj-00468-DUTY] (Entered: 03/01/2012)
02/27/2012	16	ORDER OF DETENTION by Magistrate Judge Charles F. Eick as to Defendant ███ ███████████ [2:12-mj-00468-DUTY] (Entered: 03/01/2012)
02/27/2012	17	NOTICE DIRECTING DEFENDANT TO APPEAR for Preliminary Hearing and Arraignment on Indictment/Information. Defendant ███████████████ is directed to appear for Preliminary Hearing on 3/12/12 at 4:30 P.M. and for Post Indictment Arraignment on 3/19/12 at 8:30 A.M. before the Duty Magistrate Judge. (ja) [2:12-mj-00468-DUTY] (Entered: 03/01/2012)
02/27/2012	29	FINANCIAL AFFIDAVIT filed as to Defendant ████████████████ (mhe) [2:12-mj-00468-DUTY] (Entered: 03/01/2012)
02/27/2012	2	REPORT COMMENCING CRIMINAL ACTION as to Defendant Jose Magallanes-Arias; defendant's Year of Birth: 1992; date of arrest: 2/23/2012 (ja) [2:12-mj-00468-DUTY] (Entered: 02/29/2012)
02/27/2012	3	MINUTES OF INITIAL APPEARANCE ON LOCAL COMPLAINT held before Magistrate Judge Charles F. Eick Defendant arraigned and advised of the charges. Defendant states true name as charged. Attorney: Michael S Chernis for ███ ████████████, Appointed, present. Court orders defendant permanently detained. Defendant remanded to the custody of the U.S. Marshal. Preliminary Hearing set for 3/12/2012 04:30 PM before Duty Magistrate Judge. Post-Indictment Arraignment set for 3/19/2012 08:30 AM before Duty Magistrate Judge. (SPANISH) INTERPRETER Required Court Smart: CS 2/27/12. (ja) [2:12-mj-00468-DUTY] (Entered: 03/01/2012)
02/27/2012	4	NOTICE OF REQUEST FOR DETENTION filed by Plaintiff USA as to Defendant ██████████████ (ja) [2:12-mj-00468-DUTY] (Entered: 03/01/2012)

02/27/2012	5	ORDER OF DETENTION by Magistrate Judge Charles F. Eick as to Defendant ███████ ████████████ ja) [2:12-mj-00468-DUTY] (Entered: 03/01/2012)
02/27/2012	6	NOTICE DIRECTING DEFENDANT TO APPEAR for Preliminary Hearing and Arraignment on Indictment/Information. Defendant Jose Magallanes-Arias is directed to appear for Preliminary Hearing on 3/12/12 at 4:30 P.M. and for Post Indictment Arraignment on 3/19/12 at 8:30 A.M. before the Duty Magistrate Judge. (ja) [2:12-mj-00468-DUTY] (Entered: 03/01/2012)
02/27/2012	7	ABSTRACT OF COURT PROCEEDING Issued by Magistrate Judge Charles F. Eick as to ███████████████ Recommended that the defendant be housed or designated to MDCLA. (ja) [2:12-mj-00468-DUTY] (Entered: 03/01/2012)
02/27/2012	28	FINANCIAL AFFIDAVIT filed as to Defendant J███████████████. (mhe) [2:12-mj-00468-DUTY] (Entered: 03/01/2012)
02/28/2012	18	NOTICE OF MOTION AND MOTION to Designate as Material Witness, ████ ██ ██ mhe) [2:12-mj-00468-DUTY] (Entered: 03/01/2012)
02/28/2012	19	ORDER by Magistrate Judge Margaret A. Nagle: granting 18 Motion to Designate ████████████████████████████████ as Material Witness as to Jose Magallanes-Arias (1) ███████████████████████) (mhe) [2:12-mj-00468-DUTY] (Entered: 03/01/2012)
02/28/2012	20	COMMITMENT AND ORDER by Magistrate Judge Margaret A. Nagle specifying that the material witness be incarcerated at a detention facility specially designated for illegal aliens, as place of confinement as to Material Witness ███████████ Gomez. (mhe) [2:12-mj-00468-DUTY] (Entered: 03/01/2012)
02/28/2012	21	MINUTES OF INITIAL APPEARANCE - MATERIAL WITNESS held before Magistrate Judge Margaret A. Nagle as to Material Witness Gregorio Lopez-Gomez, Adolfo Pina-Mejia, Francisco Cruz-Mencinas, Jose Herrera-Lopez, Mario Garcia-Cortez. Attorney: Special Appearance by John Littrell, DFPD, for Charles C Brown for Mario Garcia-Cortez,Charles C Brown for Jose Herrera-Lopez,Charles C Brown for Francisco Cruz-Mencinas,Charles C Brown for Adolfo Pina-Mejia,Charles C Brown for Gregorio Lopez-Gomez, Deputy Federal Public Defender, present. Court orders bail set as: $5,000 Appearance Bond, see attached bond for terms and conditions. Material Witness remanded to the custody of the U.S. Marshal., (SPANISH) INTERPRETER Required Court Smart: CS 2/28/12. (mhe) [2:12-mj-00468-DUTY] (Entered: 03/01/2012)
02/28/2012	22	COMMITMENT AND ORDER by Magistrate Judge Margaret A. Nagle specifying that the material witness be incarcerated at a detention facility specially designated for illegal aliens, as place of confinement as to Material Witness Adolfo-Pina-Mejia. (mhe)[2:12-mj-00468-DUTY] (Entered: 03/01/2012)
02/28/2012	23	COMMITMENT AND ORDER by Magistrate Judge Margaret A. Nagle specifying a detention facility specially designated for illegal aliens as place of confinement as to Material Witness Francisco Cruz-Mencinas. (ja) [2:12-mj-00468-DUTY] (Entered: 03/01/2012)

02/28/2012	24	COMMITMENT AND ORDER by Magistrate Judge Margaret A. Nagle specifying a detention facility specially designated for illegal aliens as place of confinement as to Material Witness Jose Herrera-Lopez. (ja) [2:12-mj-00468-DUTY] (Entered: 03/01/2012)
02/28/2012	25	COMMITMENT AND ORDER by Magistrate Judge Margaret A. Nagle specifying a detention facility specially designated for illegal aliens as place of confinement as to Material Witness ▮▮▮▮▮▮. (ja) [2:12-mj-00468-DUTY] (Entered: 03/01/2012)
02/28/2012	26	BOND AND CONDITIONS OF RELEASE filed as to Material Witness, Adolfo Pina-Mejia conditions of release: $5,000 Appearance Bond - SEE ATTACHED BOND FOR TERMS AND CONDITIONS approved by Magistrate Judge Margaret A. Nagle (ja) [2:12-mj-00468-DUTY] (Entered: 03/01/2012)
02/28/2012	30	FINANCIAL AFFIDAVIT filed as to Material Witness ▮▮▮▮▮▮ (ja) [2:12-mj-00468-DUTY] (Entered: 03/01/2012)
02/28/2012	31	FINANCIAL AFFIDAVIT filed as to Material Witness ▮▮▮▮ a) [2:12-mj-00468-DUTY] (Entered: 03/01/2012)
02/28/2012	32	FINANCIAL AFFIDAVIT filed as to Material Witness ▮▮▮▮▮ (ja) [2:12-mj-00468-DUTY] (Entered: 03/01/2012)
02/28/2012	33	FINANCIAL AFFIDAVIT filed as to Material Witness ▮▮▮▮ (ja) [2:12-mj-00468-DUTY] (Entered: 03/01/2012)
02/28/2012	34	FINANCIAL AFFIDAVIT filed as to Material Witness ▮▮▮▮ (ja) [2:12-mj-00468-DUTY] (Entered: 03/01/2012)
02/28/2012	35	AFFIDAVIT OF SURETIES (No Justification - Pursuant to Local Criminal Rule 46-5.2.8) in the amount of $ 5,000 by surety: Ruben Sanchez Galvez for Bond and Conditions (CR-1) - Material Witness Adolfo Pina-Mejia 26 . (ja) [2:12-mj-00468-DUTY] (Entered: 03/01/2012)
02/29/2012	36	BOND AND CONDITIONS OF RELEASE filed as to Material Witness, Gregorio Lopez-Gomez conditions of release: $5,000 Appearance Bond - SEE ATTACHED BOND FOR TERMS AND CONDITIONS approved by Magistrate Judge John E. McDermott (ja) [2:12-mj-00468-DUTY] (Entered: 03/01/2012)
02/29/2012	37	BOND AND CONDITIONS OF RELEASE filed as to Material Witness, Jose Herrera-Lopez conditions of release: $5,000 Appearance Bond - SEE ATTACHED BOND FOR TERMS AND CONDITIONS approved by Magistrate Judge John E. McDermott (ja) [2:12-mj-00468-DUTY] (Entered: 03/01/2012)
02/29/2012	38	AFFIDAVIT OF SURETIES (No Justification - Pursuant to Local Criminal Rule 46-5.2.8) in the amount of $ 5,000 by surety: Agustina Carina Gomez for Bond and Conditions (CR-1) - Material Witness only 36 . Filed by Defendants Jose Magallanes-Arias, Luis Gerardo Sanchez-Serrano, Juan Ramirez-Layva (mhe) [2:12-mj-00468-DUTY] (Entered: 03/01/2012)
02/29/2012	39	AFFIDAVIT OF SURETIES (No Justification - Pursuant to Local Criminal Rule 46-5.2.8) in the amount of $ 5,000 Appearance Bond by surety: Rajnita Rapp for Bond and Conditions (CR-1) - Material Witness Jose Herrera-Lopez 37 . (ja) [2:12-mj-00468-DUTY] (Entered: 03/01/2012)

03/02/2012	41	NOTICE OF MOTION AND MOTION to Designate and detain as Material Witnesses Cristina Lopez-San Augustin, Honoria Garcia-Cortes, Jose Juarez Falcon, Modesto Hernandez-Hernandez, Juan Gonzalez-Aguilar, Erasmo Santiano-Martinez, Jose Manuel Quinones-Rodriguez Ivan Arturo Rizo-Ledezma, Israel Dominguez-Chavez, Juan Lopez-Garcia, Amadeo Martinez-Martinez Filed by Plaintiff USA (ja) [2:12-mj-00468-DUTY] (Entered: 03/08/2012)
03/02/2012	42	ORDER by Magistrate Judge Charles F. Eick granting 41 Motion to Designate and detain Cristina Lopez-San Augustin, Honoria Garcia-Cortes, Jose Juarez Falcon, Modesto Hernandez-Hernandez, Juan Gonzalez-Aguilar, Erasmo Santiano-Martinez, Jose Manuel Quinones-Rodriguez Ivan Arturo Rizo-Ledezma, Israel Dominguez-Chavez, Juan Lopez-Garcia, Amadeo Martinez-Martinez as Material Witnesses (ja) [2:12-mj-00468-DUTY] (Entered: 03/08/2012)
03/02/2012	43	MINUTES OF INITIAL APPEARANCE - MATERIAL WITNESS held before Magistrate Judge Charles F. Eick as to Material Witnesses Cristina Lopez-San Augustin, Honoria Garcia-Cortes, Jose Juarez Falcon, Modesto Hernandez-Hernandez, Juan Gonzalez-Aguilar, Erasmo Santiano-Martinez, Jose Manuel Quinones-Rodriguez Ivan Arturo Rizo-Ledezma, Israel Dominguez-Chavez, Juan Lopez-Garcia, Amadeo Martinez-Martinez. Federal Public Defender as Counsel for Cristina Lopez-San Augustin, Honoria Garcia-Cortes, Jose Juarez Falcon, Modesto Hernandez-Hernandez, Juan Gonzalez-Aguilar, Erasmo Santiano-Martinez, Jose Manuel Quinones-Rodriguez Ivan Arturo Rizo-Ledezma, Israel Dominguez-Chavez, Juan Lopez-Garcia, Amadeo Martinez-Martinez, present. Court orders bail set as: $5,000 Appearance Bond, SEE INDIVIDUAL BOND FOR TERMS AND CONDITIONS. Status Conference Re Bond as to Juan Lopez-Garcia is set for 3/5/2012 03:00 PM before Magistrate Judge Charles F. Eick. (SPANISH) INTERPRETER Required Court Smart: CS 3/2/12. (ja) [2:12-mj-00468-DUTY] (Entered: 03/08/2012)
03/02/2012	44	COMMITMENT AND ORDER by Magistrate Judge Charles F. Eick specifying specifying a detention facility specially designated for illegal aliens as place of confinement as to Material Witness Amadeo Martinez-Martinez. (ja) [2:12-mj-00468-DUTY] (Entered: 03/08/2012)
03/02/2012	45	COMMITMENT AND ORDER by Magistrate Judge Charles F. Eick specifying specifying a detention facility specially designated for illegal aliens as place of confinement as to Material Witness Ivan Arturo Rizo-Ledezma. (ja) [2:12-mj-00468-DUTY] (Entered: 03/08/2012)
03/02/2012	46	COMMITMENT AND ORDER by Magistrate Judge Charles F. Eick specifying specifying a detention facility specially designated for illegal aliens as place of confinement as to Material Witness Israel Dominguez-Chavez. (ja) [2:12-mj-00468-DUTY] (Entered: 03/08/2012)
03/02/2012	47	COMMITMENT AND ORDER by Magistrate Judge Charles F. Eick specifying specifying a detention facility specially designated for illegal aliens as place of confinement as to Material Witness Jose Manuel Quinones-Rodriguez. (ja) [2:12-mj-00468-DUTY] (Entered: 03/08/2012)
03/02/2012	48	COMMITMENT AND ORDER by Magistrate Judge Charles F. Eick specifying specifying a detention facility specially designated for illegal aliens as place of confinement as to Material Witness Erasmo Santiano-Martinez. (ja) [2:12-mj-00468-

		DUTY] (Entered: 03/08/2012)
03/02/2012	49	COMMITMENT AND ORDER by Magistrate Judge Charles F. Eick specifying specifying a detention facility specially designated for illegal aliens as place of confinement as to Material Witness Juan Gonzalez-Aguilar. (ja) [2:12-mj-00468-DUTY] (Entered: 03/08/2012)
03/02/2012	50	COMMITMENT AND ORDER by Magistrate Judge Charles F. Eick specifying specifying a detention facility specially designated for illegal aliens as place of confinement as to Material Witness Modesto Hernandez-Hernandez. (ja) [2:12-mj-00468-DUTY] (Entered: 03/08/2012)
03/02/2012	51	COMMITMENT AND ORDER by Magistrate Judge Charles F. Eick specifying specifying a detention facility specially designated for illegal aliens as place of confinement as to Material Witness Jose Juarez Falcon. (ja) [2:12-mj-00468-DUTY] (Entered: 03/08/2012)
03/02/2012	52	COMMITMENT AND ORDER by Magistrate Judge Charles F. Eick specifying specifying a detention facility specially designated for illegal aliens as place of confinement as to Material Witness Honoria Garcia-Cortes. (ja) [2:12-mj-00468-DUTY] (Entered: 03/08/2012)
03/02/2012	53	COMMITMENT AND ORDER by Magistrate Judge Charles F. Eick specifying specifying a detention facility specially designated for illegal aliens as place of confinement as to Material Witness Cristina Lopez-San Augustin. (ja) [2:12-mj-00468-DUTY] (Entered: 03/08/2012)
03/02/2012	54	COMMITMENT AND ORDER by Magistrate Judge Charles F. Eick specifying specifying a detention facility specially designated for illegal aliens as place of confinement as to Material Witness Juan Lopez-Garcia. (ja) [2:12-mj-00468-DUTY] (Entered: 03/08/2012)
03/02/2012	55	BOND AND CONDITIONS OF RELEASE filed as to Material Witness, Israel Dominguez-Chavez conditions of release: $5,000 Appearance Bond - SEE ATTACHED BOND FOR TERMS AND CONDITIONS approved by Magistrate Judge Charles F. Eick (ja) [2:12-mj-00468-DUTY] (Entered: 03/08/2012)
03/02/2012	56	BOND AND CONDITIONS OF RELEASE filed as to Material Witness, Ivan Arturo Rizo-Ledezma conditions of release: $5,000 Appearance Bond - SEE ATTACHED BOND FOR TERMS AND CONDITIONS approved by Magistrate Judge Charles F. Eick (ja) [2:12-mj-00468-DUTY] (Entered: 03/08/2012)
03/02/2012	57	BOND AND CONDITIONS OF RELEASE filed as to Material Witness, Juan Gonzalez-Aguilar conditions of release: $5,000 Appearance Bond - SEE ATTACHED BOND FOR TERMS AND CONDITIONS approved by Magistrate Judge Charles F. Eick (ja) [2:12-mj-00468-DUTY] (Entered: 03/08/2012)
03/02/2012	58	BOND AND CONDITIONS OF RELEASE filed as to Material Witness, Cristina Lopez-San Augustin, conditions of release: $5,000 Appearance Bond - SEE ATTACHED BOND FOR TERMS AND CONDITIONS approved by Magistrate Judge Charles F. Eick (ja) [2:12-mj-00468-DUTY] (Entered: 03/08/2012)
03/02/2012	59	BOND AND CONDITIONS OF RELEASE filed as to Material Witness, Jose Manuel Quinones-Rodriguez conditions of release: $5,000 Appearance Bond - SEE ATTACHED BOND FOR TERMS AND CONDITIONS approved by Magistrate

		Judge Charles F. Eick (ja) [2:12-mj-00468-DUTY] (Entered: 03/08/2012)
03/02/2012	60	FINANCIAL AFFIDAVIT filed as to Material Witness Jose Quinones-Rodriguez (mhe) [2:12-mj-00468-DUTY] (Entered: 03/08/2012)
03/02/2012	61	FINANCIAL AFFIDAVIT filed as to Material Witness Israel Dominguez Chavez(mhe) [2:12-mj-00468-DUTY] (Entered: 03/08/2012)
03/02/2012	62	FINANCIAL AFFIDAVIT filed as to Material Witness Amadeo Martinez-Martinez(mhe) [2:12-mj-00468-DUTY] (Entered: 03/08/2012)
03/02/2012	63	FINANCIAL AFFIDAVIT filed as to Material Witness Jose Isaias Juarez Falcon (mhe) [2:12-mj-00468-DUTY] (Entered: 03/08/2012)
03/02/2012	64	FINANCIAL AFFIDAVIT filed as to Material Witness Jose Sosa-Hernandez(mhe) [2:12-mj-00468-DUTY] (Entered: 03/08/2012)
03/02/2012	65	FINANCIAL AFFIDAVIT filed as to Defendants Jose Magallanes-Arias, Luis Gerardo Sanchez-Serrano, Juan Ramirez-Layva. (mhe) [2:12-mj-00468-DUTY] (Entered: 03/08/2012)
03/02/2012	66	FINANCIAL AFFIDAVIT filed as to Material Witness Honorina Garcia-Cortes (mhe) [2:12-mj-00468-DUTY] (Entered: 03/08/2012)
03/02/2012	70	FINANCIAL AFFIDAVIT filed as to Material Witness Cristina Lopez-San Augustin (ja) [2:12-mj-00468-DUTY] (Entered: 03/09/2012)
03/02/2012	71	AFFIDAVIT OF SURETIES (No Justification - Pursuant to Local Criminal Rule 46-5.2.8) in the amount of $ 5,000 by surety: Shawnodesa Starr Luke for Bond and Conditions (CR-1) - Material Witness Israel Dominguez-Chavez 55 . (ja) [2:12-mj-00468-DUTY] (Entered: 03/09/2012)
03/02/2012	72	AFFIDAVIT OF SURETIES (No Justification - Pursuant to Local Criminal Rule 46-5.2.8) in the amount of $ 5,000 by surety: Irma Adriana Portillo Lopez for Bond and Conditions (CR-1) - Material Witness Ivan Arturo Rizo-Ledezma 56 . (ja) [2:12-mj-00468-DUTY] (Entered: 03/09/2012)
03/02/2012	73	AFFIDAVIT OF SURETIES (No Justification - Pursuant to Local Criminal Rule 46-5.2.8) in the amount of $ 5,000 by surety: Maria Del Carmen Gonzalez for Bond and Conditions (CR-1) - Material Witness Juan Gonzalez-Aguilar 57 . (ja) [2:12-mj-00468-DUTY] (Entered: 03/09/2012)
03/02/2012	75	AFFIDAVIT OF SURETIES (No Justification - Pursuant to Local Criminal Rule 46-5.2.8) in the amount of $ 5,000 by surety: Veronica Corona for Material Witness Modesto Hernandez-Hernandez (ja) [2:12-mj-00468-DUTY] (Entered: 03/09/2012)
03/02/2012	77	FINANCIAL AFFIDAVIT filed as to Material Witness Modesto Hernandez-Hernandez (ja) [2:12-mj-00468-DUTY] (Entered: 03/09/2012)
03/02/2012	78	FINANCIAL AFFIDAVIT filed as to Material Witness Juan Lopez-Garcia (ja) [2:12-mj-00468-DUTY] (Entered: 03/09/2012)
03/02/2012	79	FINANCIAL AFFIDAVIT filed as to Material Witness Juan Gonzalez-Aguilar (ja) [2:12-mj-00468-DUTY] (Entered: 03/09/2012)
03/02/2012	80	AFFIDAVIT OF SURETIES (No Justification - Pursuant to Local Criminal Rule 46-5.2.8) in the amount of $ 5,000 by surety: Irma Adriana Portillo Lopez for Bond and

		Conditions (CR-1) - Material Witness only Jose Manuel Quinones-Rodriguez <u>59</u> (ja) [2:12-mj-00468-DUTY] (Entered: 03/09/2012)
03/02/2012	<u>81</u>	AFFIDAVIT OF SURETIES (No Justification - Pursuant to Local Criminal Rule 46-5.2.8) in the amount of $ 5,000 by surety: Jacobo Martinez Perez for Material Witness Francisco Cruz Mencinas (ja) [2:12-mj-00468-DUTY] (Entered: 03/09/2012)
03/02/2012	<u>84</u>	BOND AND CONDITIONS OF RELEASE filed as to Material Witness, Modesto Hernandez-Hernandez conditions of release: $5,000 Appearance Bond - SEE ATTACHED BOND FOR TERMS AND CONDITIONS approved by Magistrate Judge Charles F. Eick (ja) [2:12-mj-00468-DUTY] (Entered: 03/09/2012)
03/02/2012	<u>86</u>	BOND AND CONDITIONS OF RELEASE filed as to Material Witness, Francisco Cruz-Mencinas conditions of release: $5,000 Appearance Bond - SEE ATTACHED BOND FOR TERMS AND CONDITIONS approved by Magistrate Judge Charles F. Eick (ja) [2:12-mj-00468-DUTY] (Entered: 03/09/2012)
03/05/2012	<u>40</u>	BOND AND CONDITIONS OF RELEASE filed as to Material Witness, Mario Garcia-Cortez conditions of release: $5,000 Appearance Bond - SEE ATTACHED BOND FOR TERMS AND CONDITIONS approved by Magistrate Judge Michael R. Wilner (ja) [2:12-mj-00468-DUTY] (Entered: 03/07/2012)
03/05/2012	<u>67</u>	AFFIDAVIT OF SURETIES (No Justification - Pursuant to Local Criminal Rule 46-5.2.8) in the amount of $ 5,000 by surety: Lidia Lopez Garcia for Material Witness Juan Lopez Garcia (ja) [2:12-mj-00468-DUTY] (Entered: 03/09/2012)
03/05/2012	<u>68</u>	AFFIDAVIT OF SURETIES (No Justification - Pursuant to Local Criminal Rule 46-5.2.8) in the amount of $ 5,000 by surety: Francisco Aguilar for Material Witness Amadeo Martinez Martinez (ja) [2:12-mj-00468-DUTY] (Entered: 03/09/2012)
03/05/2012	<u>74</u>	AFFIDAVIT OF SURETIES (No Justification - Pursuant to Local Criminal Rule 46-5.2.8) in the amount of $ 5,000 by surety: Gaspar Morales for Bond and Conditions (CR-1) - Material Witness Cristina Lopez-San Augustin <u>58</u> . (ja) [2:12-mj-00468-DUTY] (Entered: 03/09/2012)
03/05/2012	<u>76</u>	AFFIDAVIT OF SURETIES (No Justification - Pursuant to Local Criminal Rule 46-5.2.8) in the amount of $ 5,000 by surety: Honoria Garcia-Cortes for Honoria Garcia-Cortes (ja) [2:12-mj-00468-DUTY] (Entered: 03/09/2012)
03/05/2012	<u>82</u>	BOND AND CONDITIONS OF RELEASE filed as to Material Witness, Juan Lopez-Garcia conditions of release: $5,000 Appearance Bond - SEE ATTACHED BOND FOR TERMS AND CONDITIONS approved by Magistrate Judge Michael R. Wilner (ja) [2:12-mj-00468-DUTY] (Entered: 03/09/2012)
03/05/2012	<u>83</u>	BOND AND CONDITIONS OF RELEASE filed as to Material Witness, Amadeo Martinez-Martinez conditions of release: $5,000 Appearance Bond - SEE ATTACHED BOND FOR TERMS AND CONDITIONS approved by Magistrate Judge Michael R. Wilner (ja) [2:12-mj-00468-DUTY] (Entered: 03/09/2012)
03/05/2012	<u>85</u>	BOND AND CONDITIONS OF RELEASE filed as to Material Witness, Honoria Garcia-Cortes conditions of release: $5,000 Appearance Bond - SEE ATTACHED BOND FOR TERMS AND CONDITIONS approved by Magistrate Judge Charles F. Eick (ja) [2:12-mj-00468-DUTY] (Entered: 03/09/2012)

03/06/2012	69	AFFIDAVIT OF SURETIES (No Justification - Pursuant to Local Criminal Rule 46-5.2.8) in the amount of $ 5,000 by surety: Alfredo Vasquez for Bond and Conditions (CR-1) - Material Witness only 40 . (ja) [2:12-mj-00468-DUTY] (Entered: 03/09/2012)
03/07/2012	87	SEALED DOCUMENT - EXPARTE APPLICATION to File Material Witness's Supplemental Filing Re: Requirements for Release on Bond(ja) [2:12-mj-00468-DUTY] (Entered: 03/09/2012)
03/07/2012	88	SEALED DOCUMENT - ORDER GRANTING Ex Parte Application to Seal Material Witness's Supplemental Filing Re: Requirements for Release on Bond (ja) [2:12-mj-00468-DUTY] (Entered: 03/09/2012)
03/07/2012	89	SEALED DOCUMENT - SUPPLEMENTAL FILING RE: Requirements for Release on Bond (ja) (Additional attachment(s) added on 3/9/2012: # 1 Supplement Part 2) (ja). [2:12-mj-00468-DUTY] (Entered: 03/09/2012)
03/09/2012	90	INDICTMENT Filed as to Jose Magallanes-Arias (1) count(s) 1, 2-17, 18-33, Luis Gerardo Sanchez-Serrano (2) count(s) 1, 2-17, 18-33, Juan Ramirez-Layva (3) count(s) 1, 2-17, 18-33. Offense occurred in VEN. (ja) (Entered: 03/12/2012)
03/09/2012	91	CASE SUMMARY filed by AUSA Christina T. Shay as to Defendant Jose Magallanes-Arias; defendant's Year of Birth: 1992 (ja) (Entered: 03/12/2012)
03/09/2012	92	CASE SUMMARY filed by AUSA Christina T. Shay as to Defendant Luis Gerardo Sanchez-Serrano; defendant's Year of Birth: 1978 (ja) (Entered: 03/12/2012)
03/09/2012	93	CASE SUMMARY filed by AUSA Christina T. Shay as to Defendant Juan Ramirez-Layva; defendant's Year of Birth: 1987 (ja) (Entered: 03/12/2012)
03/13/2012	94	STIPULATION for Order REGARDING PROPOSED MODIFICATION OF BOND AND BOND CONDITIONS OF MATERIAL WITNESS *ERASMO SANTIANO-MARTINEZ* filed by Plaintiff Erasmo Santiano-Martinez as to Defendant Jose Magallanes-Arias, Luis Gerardo Sanchez-Serrano, Juan Ramirez-Layva (Attachments: # 1 Proposed Order)(Mehta, Neha) (Entered: 03/13/2012)
03/13/2012	95	ORDER REGARDING MODIFICATION OF BOND AND BOND CONDITIONS OF MATERIAL WITNESS by Magistrate Judge Charles F. Eick GRANTING Stipulation for Order, 94 . (mhe) (Entered: 03/15/2012)
03/13/2012	96	BOND AND CONDITIONS OF RELEASE filed as to Material Witness, Jose Juares-Falcon conditions of release: $5,000 Unsecured Appearance Bond, see attached bond for terms and conditions approved by Magistrate Judge Michael R. Wilner (mhe) (Entered: 03/15/2012)
03/19/2012	97	STATEMENT OF CONSTITUTIONAL RIGHTS filed by Defendant Luis Gerardo Sanchez-Serrano (tba) (Entered: 03/20/2012)
03/19/2012	98	STATEMENT OF CONSTITUTIONAL RIGHTS filed by Defendant Jose Magallanes-Arias (tba) (Entered: 03/20/2012)
03/19/2012	99	STATEMENT OF CONSTITUTIONAL RIGHTS filed by Defendant Juan Ramirez-Layva (tba) (Entered: 03/20/2012)
03/19/2012	100	MINUTES OF POST-INDICTMENT ARRAIGNMENT: held before Magistrate Judge Margaret A. Nagle as to Defendant Jose Magallanes-Arias (1) Count 1,2-

		17,18-33 and Luis Gerardo Sanchez-Serrano (2) Count 1,2-17,18-33 and Juan Ramirez-Layva (3) Count 1,2-17,18-33. Defendant arraigned, states true name: As charged. Defendant entered not guilty plea to all counts as charged. Attorney: 1.) Michael S. Chernis, special appearance by Paul E. Potter for 1.) Jose Magallanes-Arias, 2.) Paul E. Potter for 2.) Luis Gerardo Sanchez-Serrano, 3.) Richard P. Lasting for 3.) Juan Ramirez-Layva, Appointed present. Case assigned to Judge George H. Wu.(Jury Trial set for 4/17/2012 08:30 AM before Judge George H Wu., Status Conference set for 3/29/2012 08:00 AM before Judge George H Wu.), (Spanish) INTERPRETER Required Court Smart: CS03/19/2012. (tba) (Entered: 03/20/2012)
03/20/2012		TEXT ONLY ENTRY (IN CHAMBERS) by Judge George H Wu as to Defendant Jose Magallanes-Arias, Luis Gerardo Sanchez-Serrano, Juan Ramirez-Layva; Counsel are reminded of: Status Conference set for 3/29/2012 08:00 AM and Jury Trial set for 4/17/2012 08:30 AM before Judge George H Wu. THERE IS NO PDF DOCUMENT ASSOCIATED WITH THIS ENTRY.(jag) TEXT ONLY ENTRY (Entered: 03/20/2012)
03/20/2012	101	MODIFIED BOND AND CONDITIONS OF RELEASE filed as to Material Witness, Erasmo Santiano-Martinez conditions of release: $5,000 Appearance Bond - SEE ATTACHED BOND FOR TERMS AND CONDITIONS approved by Magistrate Judge Charles F. Eick (ja) (Entered: 03/21/2012)
03/20/2012	102	MEMORANDUM FOR RELEASE ORDER AUTHORIZATION filed by PSA Officer as to Material Witness Erasmo Santiano-Martinez, submitted in compliance with conditions as set forth in Bond and Conditions (CR-1) - Material Witness only 101 . (ja) (Entered: 03/21/2012)
03/22/2012		FINANCIAL ENTRY as to Material Witness Erasmo Santiano-Martinez: Received $5,000.00 into the registry of the Court from Felix Sanchez under case# 212MJ000468. Re: Bond and Conditions (CR-1) - Material Witness only 101 . (cma) (Entered: 03/22/2012)
03/23/2012	103	JOINT STATEMENT CONCERNING DISCOVERY filed by Plaintiff USA as to Defendant Jose Magallanes-Arias, Luis Gerardo Sanchez-Serrano, Juan Ramirez-Layva (Shay, Christina) (Entered: 03/23/2012)
03/29/2012	104	MINUTES OF Status Conference held before Judge George H Wu as to Defendant Jose Magallanes-Arias, Luis Gerardo Sanchez-Serrano, Juan Ramirez-Layva. The Jury Trial is continued to July 31, 2012 at 8:30 a.m. Pretrial Conference is set for June 18, 2012 at 8:00 a.m. Each individual defendant and their counsel orally waive their speedy trial rights on the record. A stipulation and proposed order re findings regarding excludable time periods pursuant to Speedy Trial Act will be filed forthwith Court Reporter: Pat Cuneo. (pj) (Entered: 03/30/2012)
04/05/2012	105	STIPULATION to Continue (1) TRIAL DATE and (2) FINDINGS OF EXCLUDABLE TIME PERIODS from APRIL 17, 2012 to JULY 31, 2012 filed by Plaintiff USA as to Defendant Jose Magallanes-Arias, Luis Gerardo Sanchez-Serrano, Juan Ramirez-Layva (Attachments: # 1 Proposed Order)(Shay, Christina) (Entered: 04/05/2012)
04/09/2012	106	ORDER CONTINUING TRIAL DATE AND FINDINGS REGARDING EXCLUDABLE TIME PERIODS PURSUANT TO SPEEDY TRIAL ACT by Judge George H Wu: The trial in this matter is continued from April 17, 2012, to July 31, 2012 at 8:30 a.m. The pre-trial conference hearing is continued to June 18, 2012 at

		8:00 a.m. The time period of April 17, 2012, to July 31, 2012, inclusive, is excluded in computing the time within which the trial must commence, pursuant to 18 U.S.C. §§ 3161(h)(7)(A), (h)(7)(B)(i), and (B)(iv). Under the Speedy Trial Act, the last day for trial to commence would be August 31, 2012. See order for full details. (jre) (Entered: 04/09/2012)
04/16/2012	107	NOTICE of Change of Attorney Information for attorney Charles C Brown counsel for defendants Amadeo Martinez-Martinez, Juan Lopez-Garcia, Israel Dominguez-Chavez, Ivan Arturo Rizo-Ledezma, Jose Manuel Quinones-Rodriguez.. Adding Charles C. Brown as attorney as counsel of record for Amadeo Martinez-Martinez, Juan Lopez-Garcia, Israel Dominguez-Chavez, Ivan Arturo Rizo-Ledezma, Jose Manuel Quinones-Rodriguez for the reason indicated in the G-06 Notice. Filed by defendants Amadeo Martinez-Martinez, Juan Lopez-Garcia, Israel Dominguez-Chavez, Ivan Arturo Rizo-Ledezma, Jose Manuel Quinones-Rodriguez. (Brown, Charles) (Entered: 04/16/2012)
04/16/2012	108	NOTICE of Change of Attorney Information for attorney Charles C Brown counsel for material witnesses Juan Gonzalez-Aguilar, Modesto Hernandez-Hernandez, Jose Juarez Falcon, Honoria Garcia-Cortes, Cristina Lopez-San Augustin. Adding Charles C. Brown as attorney as counsel of record for Juan Gonzalez-Aguilar, Modesto Hernandez-Hernandez, Jose Juarez Falcon, Honoria Garcia-Cortes, Cristina Lopez-San Augustin for the reason indicated in the G-06 Notice. Filed by material witnesses Juan Gonzalez-Aguilar, Modesto Hernandez-Hernandez, Jose Juarez Falcon, Honoria Garcia-Cortes, Cristina Lopez-San Augustin (Brown, Charles) (Entered: 04/16/2012)
04/17/2012	109	NOTICE of Change of Attorney Information for attorney Neha A Mehta counsel for material witness Erasmo Santiano-Martinez.Neha Mehta is no longer attorney of record for the aforementioned party in this case for the reason indicated in the G-06 Notice. Filed by material witness Erasmo Santiano-Martinez (Mehta, Neha) (Entered: 04/17/2012)
04/18/2012	110	NOTICE of Change of Attorney Information for attorney Charles C Brown counsel for material witness Erasmo Santiano-Martinez. Adding Charles C. Brown as attorney as counsel of record for Erasmo Santiano-Martinez for the reason indicated in the G-06 Notice. Filed by material witness Erasmo Santiano-Martinez (Brown, Charles) (Entered: 04/18/2012)
05/02/2012	111	EX PARTE APPLICATION for Order for BOND MODIFICATION FOR MATERIAL WITNESS IVAN ARTURO RIZO-LEDEZMA Filed by Plaintiff Ivan Arturo Rizo-Ledezma as to Defendant Jose Magallanes-Arias, Luis Gerardo Sanchez-Serrano, Juan Ramirez-Layva (Attachments: # 1 Proposed Order)(Brown, Charles) Modified on 5/10/2012 (pj). (Entered: 05/02/2012)
05/02/2012	112	EX PARTE APPLICATION for Order for BOND MODIFICATION FOR MATERIAL WITNESS ERASMO SANTIANO MARTINEZ Filed by Plaintiff Erasmo Santiano-Martinez as to Defendant Jose Magallanes-Arias, Luis Gerardo Sanchez-Serrano, Juan Ramirez-Layva (Attachments: # 1 Proposed Order)(Brown, Charles) (Entered: 05/02/2012)
05/08/2012	113	ORDER MODIFYING BOND by Judge George H Wu: GOOD CAUSE APPEARING, it is ordered that Mr. Santiano Martinez be released under the standard terms and conditions of material witness supervision, including a $5000 affidavit of surety signed by a third party approved by Pretrial Services and all other standard

		terms and conditions of material witness bond as to Jose Magallanes-Arias (1), Luis Gerardo Sanchez-Serrano (2), Juan Ramirez-Layva (3) 112 (pj) Modified on 5/10/2012 (pj). (Entered: 05/10/2012)
05/08/2012	114	ORDER MODIFYING BOND by Judge George H Wu: It is ordered that Elida Sanchez be substituted as the new surety for Mr. Rizo-Ledezma. as to Jose Magallanes-Arias (1), Luis Gerardo Sanchez-Serrano (2), Juan Ramirez-Layva (3) 111 (pj) (Entered: 05/10/2012)
06/05/2012	115	BOND AND CONDITIONS OF RELEASE filed as to Material Witness, Ivan Arturo Rizo-Ledezma conditions of release: $5,000 Appearance Bond - SEE ATTACHED BOND FOR TERMS AND CONDITIONS approved by Magistrate Judge Fernando M. Olguin (ja) (Entered: 06/08/2012)
06/05/2012	116	AFFIDAVIT OF SURETIES (No Justification - Pursuant to Local Criminal Rule 46-5.2.8) in the amount of $ 5,000 by surety: Elida Sanchez for Bond and Conditions (CR-1) - Material Witness only 115 . (ja) (Entered: 06/11/2012)
06/18/2012	117	MINUTES OF Pretrial Conference held before Judge George H Wu as to Defendant Jose Magallanes-Arias, Luis Gerardo Sanchez-Serrano, Juan Ramirez-Layva, Counsel for material witnesses Charles C. Brown, DFPD, is also present. For reasons stated on the record, the Court will allow the material witness information to be released. The Pretrial Conference is continued to July 12, 2012 at 8:00 a.m. Court Reporter: Wil Wilcox. (es) (Entered: 06/19/2012)
06/28/2012	118	PLEA AGREEMENT filed by Plaintiff USA as to Defendant Juan Ramirez-Layva (Shay, Christina) (Entered: 06/28/2012)
06/28/2012	119	PLEA AGREEMENT filed by Plaintiff USA as to Defendant Luis Gerardo Sanchez-Serrano (Shay, Christina) (Entered: 06/28/2012)
06/28/2012	120	PLEA AGREEMENT filed by Plaintiff USA as to Defendant Jose Magallanes-Arias (Shay, Christina) (Entered: 06/28/2012)
07/09/2012	121	TEXT ONLY ENTRY (IN CHAMBERS) by Judge George H Wu; The time to appear at the Change of Plea hearing as to Defendant Jose Magallanes-Arias, Luis Gerardo Sanchez-Serrano, Juan Ramirez-Layva, set for July 12, 2012 has changed from 8:00 to 10:30 a.m. THERE IS NO PDF DOCUMENT ASSOCIATED WITH THIS ENTRY.(jag) TEXT ONLY ENTRY (Entered: 07/09/2012)
07/12/2012	122	MINUTES OF Change of Plea Hearing held before Judge George H Wu as to Defendant Jose Magallanes-Arias. Defendant sworn. Court questions defendant regarding the plea. The Defendant Jose Magallanes-Arias (1) pleads GUILTY to Count 22 of the Indictment. The plea is accepted. The Court ORDERS the preparation of a Presentence Report. Sentencing set for 10/1/2012 at 8:00 AM before Judge George H Wu. Court Reporter: Katherine Stride. (es) (Entered: 07/16/2012)
07/12/2012	123	MINUTES OF Change of Plea Hearing held before Judge George H Wu as to Defendant Luis Gerardo Sanchez-Serrano. Defendant sworn. Court questions defendant regarding the plea. The Defendant Luis Gerardo Sanchez-Serrano (2) pleads GUILTY to Count 21 of the Indictment. The plea is accepted. The Court ORDERS the preparation of a Presentence Report. Parties are to submit their sentencing positions by no later than September 24, 2012. Sentencing set for 10/1/2012 at 8:00 AM before Judge George H Wu. Court Reporter: Katherine Stride.

		(es) (Entered: 07/16/2012)
07/12/2012	124	MINUTES OF Change of Plea Hearing held before Judge George H Wu as to Defendant Juan Ramirez-Layva. Defendant sworn. Court questions defendant regarding the plea. The Defendant Juan Ramirez-Layva (3) pleads GUILTY to Count 21 of the Indictment. The plea is accepted. The Court ORDERS the preparation of a Presentence Report. Sentencing set for 10/1/2012 at 8:00 AM before Judge George H Wu. Court Reporter: Katherine Stride. (es) (Entered: 07/16/2012)
08/10/2012	125	STIPULATION to Continue Sentencing Hearing from October 1, 2012 to November 5, 2012 filed by Defendant Luis Gerardo Sanchez-Serrano (Attachments: # 1 Proposed Order)(Potter, Paul) (Entered: 08/10/2012)

PACER Service Center			
Transaction Receipt			
08/14/2012 12:58:58			
PACER Login:	btt677	Client Code:	
Description:	Docket Report	Search Criteria:	2:12-cr-00218-GW End date: 8/14/2012
Billable Pages:	15	Cost:	1.50

SEAN K. KENNEDY
Federal Public Defender
HILARY L. POTASHNER
Chief Deputy

AMY M. KARL
Directing Attor
Santa Ana Of
JESUS G. BERN
Directing Attor
Riverside Of

Direct Dial: (213) 894-2

March 1, 2012

TEMPORARY IDENTIFICATION LETTER

Case Number: 12-468 M

This form is identification for the above-named material witness during pendency of this case. there are any questions, comments or concerns, please contact Pretrial Services Officer Michell Ries ████████████ or Special Agent Jack Nolan at ████████████ The material witness resides at the above-noted address. The material witness' attorney, Charles Brown is a member the Federal Public Defender's Office in Los Angeles, California. The contact number to that office is (████████ You may also contact ████████. Paralegal in the Federal Public Defender's office for assistance with this matter at (213) 894-6045.

SPECIAL INSTRUCTIONS: *Contact Sr. U S P S O Michelle Ries or Federal Public Defender Material Witne Coordinator Emma Hernandez, at the numbers listed below if there are any furtl questions or problems*

Michelle T. Ries
Senior U.S. Pretrial Services Officer

Emma Hernandez, Paralegal
Material Witness Coordinator

Bureau of Democracy, Human Rights and Labor
Country Reports on Human Rights Practices for 2011
Mexico

Mexico

📄 PDF ◁ ⬛ ▢   ↗ Permalink http://www.state.gov/j/drl/rls/hrrpt/humanrightsreport/index.htm?dlid=186528

EXECUTIVE SUMMARY

Mexico is a multiparty federal republic with an elected president and bicameral legislature. Citizens elected President Felipe Calderon of the National Action Party (PAN) in 2006 to a six-year term in generally free and fair multiparty elections. Security forces reported to civilian authorities.

The most serious human rights issues in the country arose from the fight against organized crime, which involved frequent clashes between security forces and Transnational Criminal Organizations (TCOs). TCOs and gangs linked to them battled each other to establish or maintain control of trafficking routes and markets. In multiple instances, TCOs used brutal tactics against members of the public. TCOs remained the most significant perpetrator of violent crimes in the country, showing disregard for civilian casualties, engaging in human trafficking, and intimidating journalists and human rights defenders with violence and threats. Sometimes in the context of the fight against TCOs, but also at times unrelated to it, security forces reportedly engaged in unlawful killings, forced disappearances, and instances of physical abuse and torture.

The following problems also were reported during the year by the country's National Human Rights Commission (CNDH) and other sources: kidnappings; physical abuse; poor, overcrowded prison conditions; arbitrary arrest and detention; corruption and lack of transparency that engendered impunity within the judicial system; and confessions coerced through torture. Societal problems included: killings of women; domestic violence, threats and violence against journalists and social media users, leading to self-censorship in some cases; trafficking in persons; social and economic discrimination against some members of the indigenous population; and child labor.

Despite some arrests for corruption, widespread impunity for human rights abuses by officials remained a problem in both civilian and military jurisdictions.

Section 1. Respect for the Integrity of the Person, Including Freedom from:

a. Arbitrary or Unlawful Deprivation of Life

Security forces, acting both in and out of the line of duty, killed several persons during the year.

On June 17, Joaquin Figueroa Vasquez was killed in a high-speed chase in a joint operation by state and federal security forces in the state of Veracruz and presented as an alleged TCO member. The autopsy report stated that the cause of death was a bullet wound to the head. Figueroa's family claimed that this wound and the others that Figueroa sustained were evidence of torture and a subsequent execution-style killing. In collaboration with the human rights nongovernmental organization (NGO) Mexican Commission for the Defense and Promotion of Human Rights (CMDPDH), Figueroa's family submitted information regarding the case to the Inter-American Commission on Human Rights (IACHR). The CNDH was also investigating the case at year's end.

On October 28, a military court found two officers and twelve soldiers guilty of violence resulting in the killings of three individuals at a military check point in La Joya, Sinaloa, in July 2007. The sentences ranged from 16 to 40 years in prison. NGOs and the CNDH advocated on behalf of the families involved.

There were no developments in the following two high-profile cases from 2010:

In March 2010 soldiers killed two students at Monterrey Technological University. Despite a subsequent CNDH report that determined through a thorough investigation that guns were planted at the scene and evidence was tampered with, no arrest had been made at year's end.

In June 2010 the CNDH concluded that the Secretariat of National Defense (SEDENA) altered the location in which Martin and Bryan Almanza Salazar, ages five and nine, respectively, were shot and killed in April 2010 to create the impression that the shots occurred during a firefight with a criminal gang. The CNDH concluded that the children had been killed by direct fire from army troops on the road from Nuevo Laredo to Reynosa, Tamaulipas. However, military findings concluded that the children had been killed by shrapnel from a grenade thrown by members of organized criminal organizations. The incident remained under investigation at year's end.

A number of killings committed by TCOs appeared to be politically motivated. Unidentified perpetrators killed seven mayors of small towns in states along the country's northern border during the year, allegedly for failing to cooperate with organized crime. In 2010-11, a total of 20 sitting mayors were killed. Most of the killings were linked to organized crime.

Three activists from the Movement for Peace and Justice with Dignity, which sought justice for victims of drug-related violence, were allegedly killed by TCOs during the year. Nepomuceno Moreno was killed in Sonora on November 30, and Pedro Leyva Dominguez and Trinidad de la Cruz Crisostomo were killed in Michoacan on October 6 and December 7, respectively.

b. Disappearance

There were multiple reports of forced disappearances by the army, navy, and police. Most occurred in the course of security operations. In several cases of reported disappearances, security forces had detained the missing persons incommunicado for several days. Following its March visit, the UN Working Group on Enforced or Involuntary Disappearances underscored patterns of impunity and a lack of investigation in cases of forced disappearance. The working group indicated that the number of new cases it accepted more than tripled from 2010. The group noted that the increased numbers of newly admitted cases and the high number of new allegations received during the visit could indicate a worsening situation of forced disappearances in the country.

On March 26, municipal police in Ciudad Juarez, Chihuahua, allegedly detained Juan Carlos Chavira, Dante Castillo, Raul Navarro, and Felix Vizcarra. Family members of the victims found their abandoned pick-up truck on March 27 in a tunnel far from where they had been detained. On April 14, the dead bodies of the four missing men were discovered. The state prosecutor's office commented publicly that it was investigating the case as a crime of enforced disappearance. Hector Murguia Lardizabal, mayor of Ciudad Juarez, said that he had also ordered the city's police department of internal affairs to investigate the case. Three local police were arrested on April 8 and at year's end legal proceedings against them were ongoing.

In February 2010 soldiers in Chilpancingo, Guerrero, allegedly beat and took Raul Evangelista Alonso from his home. Several days later in the same city, Roberto Gonzalez Mosso was abducted by masked individuals claiming to be from the Office of the Deputy Attorney General for Special Organized Crime Investigations (SIEDO). At year's end neither individual had been seen, and information on the status of the investigation was unavailable.

Kidnapping remained a serious problem for persons of all socioeconomic levels. The government reported a 6 percent increase in kidnappings in the first half of the year compared with the same period in 2010. Many kidnapping cases continued to go unreported, as families feared repercussions and often negotiated directly with kidnappers. Informed observers believed the number of cases reported to authorities was far less than the actual number. There were credible reports of police involvement in kidnappings for ransom, primarily at the state and local level. In February a law against kidnapping went into effect that mandates harsher penalties for convicted kidnappers and the improvement of victims' services. The government continued to advance compliance with its 2008 "National Agreement on Security, Justice and Legality," which calls for the establishment of specialized, vetted antikidnapping units. At year's end 22 states had established such units.

c. Torture and Other Cruel, Inhuman, or Degrading Treatment or Punishment

The law prohibits torture and other cruel, inhuman, or degrading treatment and stipulates that confessions obtained through illicit means such as torture are not admissible as evidence in court. Similarly inadmissible is any confession made directly to police. To be admissible a confession must be formally recorded before a prosecutor with the acknowledgement that it is being made voluntarily and after examination by a doctor confirming that the person has not been subjected to physical abuse. In multiple cases, however, the CNDH verified the falsification of medical certificates to cover up torture.

During the year the CNDH received 1,626 complaints of cruel or degrading treatment and 42 torture complaints, compared with 1,170 complaints of cruel or degrading treatment and 10 torture complaints in 2010. In some instances U.S. citizens reported receiving beatings, suffocation, and administration of electric shock when in the custody of arresting authorities.

In its November 2011 report, Human Rights Watch (HRW) reported more than 170 cases of torture committed by security forces in the states of Baja California, Chihuahua, Guerrero, Nuevo Leon, and Tabasco since the beginning of the government's fight against TCOs in 2006. The report noted that the most common forms of torture included "beatings, asphyxiation with plastic bags, waterboarding, electric shocks, sexual torture, and death threats."

On August 31, the CNDH issued a recommendation regarding grave human rights violations suffered by Israel Arzate Melendez, a resident of Ciudad Juarez accused of having participated in the massacre of Villas de Salvarcar in January 2010, in which a group of young people were killed in Ciudad Juarez. Several days later soldiers reportedly detained Arzate as he was walking in the street. During the ensuing car ride and upon arrival at the 20th Motorized Cavalry Regiment in Ciudad Juarez, Arzate was allegedly beaten, tortured with electric shocks to the chest and abdomen, and asphyxiated with a plastic bag. Soldiers later said that they had detained him for being in possession of a stolen vehicle. The soldiers presented Arzate before the public prosecutor 28 hours after his detention but kept him at the military facility, where in February 2010 he was allegedly forced to confess, under torture and threats, to having participated in the killings in Villas de Salvarcar. On December 6, the Ninth District Judge of Chihuahua dismissed evidence allegedly corroborating security forces' use of torture on Arzate. According to the NGO Miguel Agustin Pro Juarez Human Rights Center (Center Prodh), Arzate remained in pretrial custody at year's end and was returned on several occasions to military custody, where he was again tortured.

The government took steps to implement preventive measures against the practice of torture, including applying, at the federal level, the Istanbul Protocol, which contains guidance on investigating and documenting torture and other abuses. According to the Attorney General's Office (PGR), 14 of the country's 31 states had passed laws to implement the protocol and established offices to evaluate allegations. Additionally the PGR reported that it had provided training on human rights and torture to its local, state, and federal staff. During the year the CNDH conducted 181 human rights–related courses for SEDENA, 49 for the PGR, and 186 for the Secretariat of Public Security (SSP). The courses included sections on torture. The CNDH made 33 visits to prisons during the year specifically to monitor the application of the Istanbul Protocol and investigate torture allegations by prisoners.

In May 2010 the UN Subcommittee on the Prevention of Torture made public the recommendations from its 2009 report and visit. The Foreign Affairs Secretariat announced in July 2010 an action plan to implement the 122 recommendations listed in the report, although it had not published information on specific actions taken by year's end.

Instances of cruel, inhuman, and degrading treatment were reported to occur in public mental health institutions, including the use of unconsented lobotomies on persons with disabilities (see section 6, Persons with Disabilities).

Prison and Detention Center Conditions

Prison conditions remained poor. During the year the CNDH and NGOs reported that corruption, overcrowding, prisoner abuse, alcoholism, and drug addiction were prevalent in most facilities. According to the CNDH, health and sanitary conditions were poor, and most prisons did not offer psychiatric care. According to accounts related to consular officers by prisoners, poorly trained, underpaid, and corrupt guards staffed most prisons, and authorities occasionally placed prisoners in solitary confinement for indefinite periods. Prisoners often had to bribe guards to acquire food, medicine, and other necessities. Prison overcrowding continued to be a common problem. According to the SSP, as of July there were 227,671 prisoners in 431 facilities in the country, which were approximately 23 percent above capacity. Approximately 217,200 (95.4 percent) of those inmates were men and 10,470 (4.6 percent) were women. The official number of juvenile inmates was unknown. In its Strategic Plan for 2008-12, the SSP described the penitentiary system as "one of the most underdeveloped and abandoned components of public security."

Prison conditions in the country varied greatly across states and facilities. There were reports of dire and at times life-threatening conditions for prisoners due to overcrowding, posing risks to the prisoners' physical safety and health. The CNDH noted that lack of access to adequate healthcare was a significant problem at all facilities. Prisoners generally had access to potable water.

The SSP reported that between July 2010 and July 2011, 52 inmates were killed in prison. The most significant prison riots during the year were caused by skirmishes between prisoners from rival gangs and cartels. In July an incident in a prison in Nuevo Laredo left seven dead and allowed 59 prisoners to escape, 35 of whom were being held on federal charges such as drug trafficking. Later that month a prison riot in Ciudad Juarez resulted in the deaths of 17 inmates. Cameras showed prisoners gaining access to cells using a guard's keys and firing what appeared to be automatic weapons at the individuals inside. On October 15, 20 prisoners died and 12 were wounded in a prison riot at Matamoros's state prison. Authorities claimed the riot was caused by feuding groups within the prison.

Pretrial detainees were routinely held together with convicted criminals. In its September report on the state of the penitentiary system, the CNDH noted that conditions for female prisoners were inferior to those for men, particularly for women who lived with their children in prison, due to a lack of appropriate living facilities and specialized medical care. There were reports that women who lived with their children in prison did not receive extra food or assistance. There were reports of physical and sexual abuse of women while in detention.

In December 2010 inmate Gabriela Elizabeth Muniz Tamez was taken from an official police vehicle by unidentified armed men allegedly belonging to a TCO while being transferred from a prison to a nearby hospital in Monterrey, Nuevo Leon. Her body, which bore signs of torture, was later found hanging from a bridge in the city.

Prisoners and detainees had reasonable access to visitors and were permitted religious observance. While prisoners and detainees were generally permitted to lodge complaints about human rights violations, access to justice was inconsistent, and the results of investigations were generally not made public.

The government permitted independent monitoring of prison conditions by the International Committee of the Red Cross (ICRC), the CNDH, and state human rights commissions. The CNDH made 153 visits to civilian and military prisons and detention centers nationwide during the year to monitor conditions. The CNDH also opened 329 complaint cases based on concerns about human rights violations against prisoners and received 235 complaints of "cruel treatment."

Independent monitors are generally limited to making recommendations to authorities to improve prison conditions. The CNDH has an ombudsman dedicated to prison issues, but the office does not provide legal representation for prisoners.

The federal government worked to improve prison conditions by implementing its 2008-12 strategic plan focused on security, rehabilitation, and education. During the year the SSP worked to improve the federal penitentiary system through programs dedicated to preparing prisoners for future employment, modernization of security equipment, standardization of norms and procedures throughout the prison system, and creation of university majors in prison administration. The SSP also finalized and implemented a new prisoner classification system and file format for offenders housed in federal prisons. In November the SSP initiated an international accreditation process to standardize facilities in the federal penitentiary system. There were no known improvements in alternatives to sentencing for nonviolent offenders during the year.

d. Arbitrary Arrest or Detention

The law prohibits arbitrary arrest and detention as well as sponsoring or covering up an illegal detention. However, the CNDH reported receiving 1,744 complaints of arbitrary arrests and detentions during the year.

Role of the Police and Security Apparatus

The federal police, under the SSP, as well as state and municipal police, have primary responsibility in law and in practice for law enforcement and the maintenance of order. SEDENA, which oversees the army and the air force, and the Secretariat of the Navy (SEMAR), which oversees the navy and the marines, also play an important role in the fight against transnational organized crime.

According to the CNDH, SEDENA was the government entity with the greatest number of human rights complaints (1,695) filed against it during the year.

The CNDH stated that deployment of the armed forces for domestic law enforcement in the struggle against TCOs led to an increased number of reported human rights abuses. The lack of clear protocol for use of force and rules of engagement worsened the problem, leading President Calderon in December 2010 to instruct military and police forces to establish protocols for the legitimate use of force. SEMAR, which played an increasingly important domestic security role, saw CNDH human rights complaints more than double from 198 in 2010 to 495 in 2011. Credible human rights NGOs continued to charge that an opaque military justice system contributed to impunity, pointing to a failure to openly and promptly investigate, prosecute, and convict members of the military for human rights violations.

The CNDH reported that police, immigration officers, and customs officials violated the rights of undocumented migrants and failed to provide for their safety. In August a Guatemalan migrant was beaten to death in Mexico State, allegedly by municipal police.

During the year the CNDH issued 25 recommendations (based on certifications that a case involved a serious human rights violation and merits further investigation or sanction) to SEDENA concerning allegations of human rights violations committed by members of the armed forces, compared with 22 in 2010. SEDENA accepted all of the recommendations and affirmed its commitment to collaborating with the CNDH on outstanding investigations. The CNDH issued six recommendations to SEMAR during the year, the same number as in 2010. The CNDH also issued six recommendations to the PGR and 15 to the SSP. All of these recommendations were accepted.

SEDENA's General Directorate for Human Rights investigates military personnel for violations of human rights identified by the CNDH and is tasked with promoting a culture of respect for human rights within the institution. However, the directorate has no power to ensure allegations are properly prosecuted. Human rights NGOs such as Center Prodh complained about a lack of access to the directorate and maintained the directorate had not improved SEDENA's human rights performance.

Despite a persistent lack of human rights-related prosecutions by military tribunals, SEDENA took steps to increase transparency on its handling of human rights cases, such as listing on its Web site the status of military trials and their compliance with CNDH recommendations.

SEDENA reported that at year's end 16 soldiers and three officers had been sentenced since 2006 for human rights-related crimes committed against civilians. Additionally, SEDENA reported that 168 soldiers were under investigation and 65 were in a military trial process for a variety of human rights offenses.

The CNDH provided human rights training to 30,108 military personnel during the year. SEDENA reported that during the year 207,829 soldiers participated in courses dedicated to human rights.

The SSP worked with the International Organization for Migration and experts from the ICRC to train federal police officers on human rights. The ICRC also provided training to military personnel on international human rights law. Additionally, the CNDH trained 10,169 SSP officials. The SSP in collaboration with the National Autonomous University of Mexico continued to provide human rights training to federal police officers throughout the country. The SSP, the Latin American Institute for Education Communication, and a foreign donor established a Masters Degree on Human Rights for SSP personnel. Separately, the CNDH provided training to 1,448 PGR personnel.

Arrest Procedures and Treatment While in Detention

By law only duly authorized officials are permitted to apprehend an individual. However, a warrant for arrest is not required if the official has reasonable suspicion about the person's involvement in a crime. Bail exists but not for persons being held in connection with drug trafficking or other forms of organized crime. In states that had not yet implemented the 2008 reforms, pretrial release on bond was available only in cases in which the charged offense was not considered a serious crime. In most cases persons must be presented to a judge, along with sufficient evidence to justify their continued detention, within 48 hours of their arrest. According to many NGOs, in practice there were violations of this 48-hour provision. The CNDH received 423 complaints involving illegal detention.

In organized crime cases (involving three or more persons who organize for the purpose of committing certain crimes), suspects may be held for up to 96 hours before being presented to a judge. Only the federal judicial system can prosecute organized crime cases. However, in recognition of the complex nature of organized crime, the constitution was amended to stipulate that, under a precautionary procedure known as "arraigo," certain suspects may, with the approval of a judge, be detained for up to 80 days prior to the filing of formal charges. In the absence of formal charges, persons so detained are not entitled to legal representation and are not eligible to receive credit for time served if convicted. During her July visit, UN High Commissioner for Human Rights Navi Pillay criticized this form of pretrial detention as a violation of due process that facilitated torture. Human rights groups, including the CMDPDH, alleged that arraigo was used to obtain forced confessions. In July the state of Chiapas declared the practice illegal.

In areas involving military operations against TCOs, SEDENA personnel detained individuals without the involvement of state or federal investigators authorized to collect evidence for use in subsequent prosecutions. The PGR claimed it was not always notified in a timely manner of the detentions, which complicated efforts to prosecute and convict arrestees.

While detainees usually were allowed prompt access to family members and to counsel, there were complaints that in some cases police held persons incommunicado for several days and made arrests arbitrarily and without a warrant. While indigent detainees are provided counsel under law, in practice counsel was generally only provided during trials and not during arrests or investigations. Detainees were sometimes held under house arrest. Human rights NGOs documented and the CNDH issued several recommendations confirming that the army frequently detained civilians for extended periods of time before placing them at the disposition of civilian authorities.

Pretrial Detention: The law provides time limits within which an accused person must be tried. However, due to caseloads that far exceeded the capacity of the federal judicial system and the fact that most state judicial systems still used the written inquisitorial criminal justice system, such time limits often were disregarded. The Mexican Center for Research and Teaching in Economics (CIDE) and HRW reported that more than 40 percent of prisoners were held in pretrial detention, as opposed to serving time for a convicted offense. Many spent years in pretrial detention. According to CIDE the average period for prisoners awaiting trial is two years and of those sentenced, 14 percent were declared innocent after having served time in prison, and 85 percent received sentences of less than five years. For many of these, the time spent in prison ultimately exceeded the sentence, according to CIDE.

e. Denial of Fair Public Trial

Although the constitution and law provide for an independent judiciary, court decisions were susceptible to improper influence by both private and public entities, particularly at the state and local level, according to CIDE. Civil society organizations reported that corruption, inefficiency, and a lack of transparency continued to be major problems in the judiciary.

International bodies, including the IACHR and the Office of the UN High Commissioner for Human Rights (OHCHR), criticized the government's failure to limit military jurisdiction over human rights cases. Article 57 of the military code of justice defines crimes against military discipline as "state or common offenses that have been committed by active duty military." In practice civilian courts generally ceded jurisdiction to the military in cases where military personnel stood accused of human rights violations committed against civilians. However, in July the Supreme Court ruled that civil courts at all levels should guide their decisions by the constitution and the country's human rights obligations under international conventions when such laws are found to conflict with other codes and norms, including Article 57 of the military justice code. President Calderon reiterated in a speech on December 10 his administration's commitment to transfer human rights crimes from military to civilian jurisdiction. At year's end two human rights cases involving the military had been transferred to civilian jurisdiction, and a Guerrero state judge had ordered that a third case also be transferred.

Trial Procedures

The civilian legal system is a hybrid system. While it incorporates some aspects of common law and accusatory-style systems, it draws primarily from traditional European code-based, inquisitorial systems. The 2008 constitutional criminal justice reforms mandated implementation of an oral adversarial system and the presumption of innocence by 2016. The military employs an inquisitorial legal system but continued to move toward an oral accusatorial system.

At year's end 12 states had passed legislation transitioning to the oral, adversarial system and were at various stages of training and implementation, and 13 states were in the process of legislating reforms. Under the old system, still being used by the federal government, federal district, and 23 states—some of which had passed reforms but were still transitioning to the new system—a typical trial consists of a series of fact-gathering hearings during which the court receives documentary evidence or testimony. A judge in chambers reviews the case file and then issues a final, written ruling. The record of the proceeding is not available to the general public, only the parties involved have access to the official file and only by special motion.

The 2008 constitutional criminal justice reform establishes that defendants enjoy a presumption of innocence. However, such rights are not provided for in jurisdictions that have not completed reform implementation and still operate under the inquisitorial system.

The constitutional reform provides for the right of the accused to attend the hearings and challenge the evidence or testimony presented, and the government generally respected these rights in practice. In most cases court proceedings were open to the public. Defendants are not tried by jury.

While the law provides defendants with the right to an attorney at all stages of criminal proceedings, in practice this only meant that authorities had to appoint a "person of confidence," who was not required to meet any particular legal qualifications to represent a defendant. Because of the nascent implementation of the 2008 reforms, not all public defenders had preparation and training to serve adequately on the defendants' behalf, and often the state public defender system was not adequate to meet demand. Public defender services were placed either in the judicial or executive branch. There were rarely autonomous public defender services. According to Amnesty International (AI) and CIDE, most criminal suspects did not receive representation until after they were placed under judicial authority, thus making individuals vulnerable to coercion to sign false statements before being presented to a judge.

Although the law provides for translation services from Spanish to indigenous languages to be available at all stages of the criminal process, NGOs noted that this generally was not done. Indigenous defendants who did not speak Spanish sometimes were unaware of the status of their cases, and some suspects were convicted without fully understanding the documents they were required to sign.

According to human rights NGOs, including HRW and AI, despite enactment of the 2008 judicial reform legislation, judges, particularly in areas that had not yet implemented the reforms, continued to allow statements coerced through torture to be used as evidence against the accused. Confessions were often the primary evidence in criminal convictions in these cases (see section 1.c.). NGOs asserted that judges often gave greater evidentiary value to the first declaration of a defendant given in the absence of legal representation, providing prosecutors an incentive to obtain an incriminating first confession. For their part law enforcement officials complained that defendants frequently made baseless claims of coerced confessions as a way to win acquittal.

The 2008 justice reform establishes strict guidelines on the use of confessions, evidence, and expert testimony; allows consensual monitoring of telephone calls; and gives police more responsibility for conducting investigations. The reform stipulates that all hearings and trials must be conducted by a judge and under the principles of public access, immediacy, confrontation, and cross-examination, promoting greater transparency and allowing defendants to challenge their accusers. The law allows the government to keep elements of an investigation confidential until evidence is presented in court, and defendants do not usually have access to government-held evidence.

Political Prisoners and Detainees

There were no reports of political prisoners or detainees.

Regional Human Rights Court Decisions

In 2009 the Inter-American Court of Human Rights issued a binding ruling calling for the country to evaluate and reform the process of using military courts to try human rights cases involving civilians. In July the Supreme Court ruled that civilian courts must maintain cases involving human rights abuses of civilians in civilian jurisdiction. In August military prosecutors declined jurisdiction over two high-profile human rights cases (see section 6, Indigenous People). The government also held public ceremonies honoring victims in accordance with three Inter-American Court rulings.

Civil Judicial Procedures and Remedies

There is an independent and impartial judiciary in civil matters to which citizens have access to seek damages for a human rights violation. However, for a plaintiff to secure damages against a defendant, the defendant first must have been found guilty in a criminal case, which was a high standard in view of the relatively low number of individuals convicted of human rights abuses in the country.

f. Arbitrary Interference with Privacy, Family, Home, or Correspondence

Although the law prohibits such practices and requires search warrants, the CNDH received 213 complaints of illegal searches or destruction of property during the year, most related to the fight against organized crime.

The NGO Tlachinollan Mountain Center for Human Rights, located in Ayutla de los Libres, Guerrero, reported instances of soldiers entering employees' homes without a warrant and appropriating personal property.

Section 2. Respect for Civil Liberties, Including:

a. Freedom of Speech and Press

Status of Freedom of Speech and Press

The law provides for freedom of speech and press, and the government generally respected these rights in practice. Most newspapers and television and radio stations were privately owned, and the government had minimal presence in the ownership of news media.

Freedom of Press: Despite federal government support for freedom of the press, many journalists were the victims of threats, harassment, and violence. Reporters covering organized crime, including its links to corrupt public officials, acknowledged practicing self-censorship, recognizing the danger investigative journalism posed to them and to their families. In their final report released in June following a country visit in 2010, the UN and Organization of American States special rapporteurs for the promotion and protection of the right to freedom of opinion and expression characterized the states of Chihuahua, Coahuila, Durango, Guerrero, Michoacan, Nuevo Leon, Sinaloa, and Tamaulipas as "completely silent" due to dramatic levels of media self-censorship.

The law does not provide a legal framework for issuing permits to nongovernmental and noncommercial community radio stations.

Violence and Harassment: According to the NGO Article 19, during the year nine journalists were killed--four in the state of Veracruz--and two disappeared, compared with nine such killings and four disappearances in 2010. The CNDH reported that 70 journalists had been killed and 13 disappeared since 2000.

The PGR's Office of the Special Prosecutor for Crimes Against Journalists accepted jurisdiction of more than 15 cases between September 2010 and June 2011. The CNDH issued three recommendations on crimes against journalists during the year.

High-profile cases included the following:

Noel Lopez Olguin, a columnist for the newspaper *La Verdad de Jaltipan* in Veracruz, was kidnapped on March 8 and found dead on May 31 in that state. His body was discovered after a drug gang member confessed to the killing. According to reports, Lopez wrote stories on corruption involving organized crime.

Two reporters from *Notiver* in Veracruz were killed during the year. Miguel Angel Lopez Velasco, a columnist for the newspaper, was found dead in his Veracruz home along with his wife and 21-year-old son on June 20. Juan Carlos "El Naca" Carranza Saavedra was named as a suspect by the state attorney general and a three million peso ($233,000) reward was offered for information leading to his arrest. Lopez's writings focused on drug trafficking and security. On July 26, the body of Yolanda Ordaz de la Cruz, a crime beat reporter for *Notiver*, was also found in Veracruz. A note left at the crime scene suggested a connection between the two killings. At year's end information on the investigations remained unavailable.

No developments were reported in the arrest and investigation of suspects associated with multiple 2010 cases of violence against journalists.

In October 2010 the government announced the launching of a journalist protection mechanism. While NGOs such as Article 19 noted that the mechanism had not been effectively implemented due to a lack of funding, insufficient consultation with civil society, and reliance on local rather than federal authorities for protection responsibilities, the government made efforts to involve civil society and work with international partners to train personnel involved in the mechanism's implementation. In a speech on December 10, President Calderon reiterated his administration's commitment to improve mechanisms to protect journalists and human rights defenders in cooperation with the CNDH and the UN. He identified organized crime as the major source of kidnapping threats and noted that the mechanism had provided protection to 11 individuals thus far.

Libel Laws/National Security: Although defamation, libel, and slander are not federal offenses, 17 states have criminal libel laws making journalists vulnerable to imprisonment at the state level.

Nongovernmental Impact: TCOs exercised an increasing influence over media outlets and reporters, at times directly threatening individuals who published critical views of crime groups.

On September 24, police in Nuevo Laredo found the headless body of a female journalist who wrote on TCO activity as an online blogger under the pseudonym of "La Nena de Laredo" ("Laredo Girl"). Two other Nuevo Laredo-based bloggers were allegedly tortured and killed by TCOs in September and November, again in retaliation for posting comments on the Internet about local drug cartels.

Internet Freedom

There were no government restrictions on access to the Internet or credible reports that the government monitored e-mail or Internet chat rooms. Individuals and groups could engage in the expression of views via the Internet, including by e-mail.

As citizens increasingly used social media Web sites such as Twitter and Facebook to obtain and share drug-related news, violence against the users of these sites rose dramatically.

Two states introduced new restrictions on the use of social media. In August Veracruz officials arrested Gilberto Martinez Vera and Maria de Jesus Bravo Pagola for allegedly spreading rumors of violence on Twitter. They were released following protests from civil society groups, but the state created a new "public disturbance" offense for use in similar cases in the future. Similarly, the state of Tabasco outlawed telephone calls or social network postings that could provoke panic. Civil society groups feared that the laws could be used to curb freedom of expression online.

Academic Freedom and Cultural Events

There were no government restrictions on academic freedom or cultural events.

b. Freedom of Peaceful Assembly and Association

The law provides for freedom of assembly and the government generally respected this right in practice. However, there was at least once instance of security forces using force against demonstrators during the year.

On December 12, approximately 500 students from the Teachers' College of Ayotzinapa in the state of Guerrero, along with members of civil society organizations, blocked traffic on an important federal highway near the state capital and demanded a meeting with the governor to discuss conditions at the school. When state and federal police attempted to dislodge the protesters and reopen the highway, both security forces and protesters resorted to violence, during which police shot and killed two protesters, and protesters set fire to a gas station, resulting in the death of a gas station employee. NGOs and the state human rights commission condemned the killings. At year's end the governor of Guerrero had fired a number of high-ranking state officials in connection with the killings, and investigations were continuing.

Freedom of Association

The law provides for freedom of association, and the government generally respected this right in practice.

c. Freedom of Religion

See the Department of State's International Religious Freedom Report at www.state.gov/j/drl/irf/rpt.

d. Freedom of Movement, Internally Displaced Persons, Protection of Refugees, and Stateless Persons

The law provides for freedom of movement within the country, foreign travel, emigration, and repatriation, and the government generally respected these rights in practice. However, according to several NGOs including AI, the army in the course of its operations occasionally restricted freedom of movement. The government cooperated with the Office of the UN High Commissioner for Refugees and other humanitarian organizations in providing protection and assistance to internally displaced persons, refugees, returning refugees, asylum seekers, stateless persons, and other persons of concern.

In-country Movement: In a February report, the CNDH estimated that approximately 11,330 migrants were kidnapped between April and September 2010 as they attempted to transit the country to cross the border into the United States, although the National Migration Institute (INM) disputed this claim, noting that they had registered only 222 such cases during the same period. Many migrants were reluctant to report such crimes due to fear of being deported.

Forty Central American migrants were abducted from a train in December 2010. Another mass kidnapping of migrants riding a train from Oaxaca to Veracruz took place in June. Both the CNDH and the INM continued to investigate the incidents at year's end.

Protection of Refugees

Access to Asylum: The country's laws provide for the granting of asylum or refugee status, and the government has established a system for providing protection to refugees.

Section 3. Respect for Political Rights: The Right of Citizens to Change Their Government

The law provides citizens the right to change their government peacefully, and citizens exercised this right in practice through periodic, free, and fair elections held on the basis of universal suffrage.

Elections and Political Participation

Recent Elections: The closely contested 2006 presidential election, in which Felipe Calderon was elected president to a six-year term, was considered generally free and fair by most neutral observers, including EU representatives and local and international civil society organizations.

Participation of Women and Minorities: As of December there were 30 women in the 128-seat Senate and 141 women in the 500-seat lower house. Two female justices sat on the 11-member Supreme Court, and there were four women in the 19-member cabinet. Many state electoral codes provide that no more than 70 to 80 percent of candidates can be of the same gender. Some political parties utilized quotas requiring that a certain percentage of candidates on a party list be female.

There were no established quotas for increased participation of indigenous groups in the legislative body, and no reliable statistics were available regarding minority participation in government. The law provides for the right of indigenous people to elect representatives to local office according to "usages and customs" law rather than federal and state electoral law. Usages and customs laws applied traditional practices to resolve disputes, chose local officials, and collected taxes without federal or state government interference. While such practices allowed communities to select officials according to their traditions, the usages and customs law generally excluded women from the political process and often infringed on the rights of women and religious minorities. The application of the law varied by village. In some villages women were not permitted to vote or hold office, in others they could vote but not hold office.

Section 4. Official Corruption and Government Transparency

The law provides criminal penalties for official corruption. However, the government did not always implement the law effectively. Credible reports indicated that officials frequently engaged in corrupt practices with impunity and that relatively few cases were brought to trial. Corruption at the most basic level involved paying bribes for routine services or in lieu of fines to administrative officials and security forces. More sophisticated and less apparent forms of corruption included overpaying for goods and services to provide payment to elected officials and political parties.

During the year the PGR initiated legal proceedings against 102 employees for corruption, 18 of whom were convicted at year's end. The INM dismissed 400 employees accused of corruption and human trafficking, 15 of whom were under PGR investigation at year's end. The state of Veracruz fired more than 1,000 police officers after they failed newly implemented vetting checks.

The CNDH reported that police, particularly at the state and local level, were involved in kidnapping, extortion, and in providing protection for, or acting directly on behalf of, organized crime and drug traffickers. Local forces in particular tended to be poorly compensated and directly pressured by criminal groups, leaving them most vulnerable to infiltration. Responsibility for investigating federal police criminal abuse falls under the purview of the PGR or the Secretariat of Public Administration, depending on the type of offense.

On December 2, Humberto Moreira, the former governor of Coahuila (2005–11) and then party leader of the Institutional Revolutionary Party (PRI), announced his resignation from party leadership amid escalating controversy over a debt scandal during his tenure as governor. In August the PGR began a criminal investigation into allegations that the state government of Coahuila had underreported its debt by almost $3 billion and had forged official documents to obtain loans. The Secretariat of Finance filed a criminal lawsuit with the PGR against the state of Coahuila, and the investigation continued at year's end.

On September 1, federal police arrested a state police officer in connection with the August 25 arson attack on a casino in Monterrey that left 52 people dead. The unidentified state officer was one of several men seen in a surveillance camera video arriving at the casino in a caravan. Some of the men rushed in to set the building on fire in what authorities suspected may have been retaliation for the casino's owners refusing to pay an extortion demand to organized criminals. At year's end at least five suspects had been detained by federal authorities and investigations continued.

In May 2010 SIEDO prosecuted Cancun Mayor Gregorio Sanchez, and a federal judge charged him with money laundering, drug trafficking, and cooperating with drug traffickers. These charges were eventually dropped. Sanchez was arrested once again in July for allegedly smuggling Cuban citizens into the country, and for additional drug allegations, but he was released in August.

Financial disclosure and accounting laws are overseen by the National Banking and Exchange Commission. In practice authorities' application of the laws was inconsistent.

Internal controls and vetting processes were applied to new SSP entrants and incrementally expanded to existing staff. The SSP managed a database of police at all levels whose records, including misdeeds, are catalogued. The SSP expanded the Intranet-based communications platform, Plataforma Mexico, allowing for communication and coordination with federal and some state and local police throughout the country. At both federal and state levels, authorities provided for the establishment of Citizen Participation Councils (CPCs) to address citizen complaints about police and other justice system actors. CPCs created "observatories" to monitor criminal justice and security issues.

Despite significant institutional and regulatory changes increasing government transparency, access to information continued to be difficult in some states. The Federal Institute of Access to Public Information (IFAI), the agency responsible for freedom of information requests, received more than 120,000 such requests during the year. All states have laws complying with the 2007 constitutional reforms regarding access to information and have signed formal agreements with IFAI to make the information system on government operations, Infomex, available for petitions for state government information.

In March the Supreme Court ruled that the PGR had the right to withhold information from the CNDH in cases that are actively under investigation. The decision was in response to the July 2010 case brought by the CNDH challenging the PGR's right to withhold information.

Section 5. Governmental Attitude Regarding International and Nongovernmental Investigation of Alleged Violations of Human Rights

A variety of domestic and international human rights groups generally operated without government restriction, investigating and publishing their findings on human rights cases. Government officials were somewhat cooperative and responsive to their views. The government made periodic attempts to engage civil society on human rights issues by encouraging participation in policy debates and engaging with victims and their family members in public discussions. President Calderon and his secretary of government engaged in public discussions on several occasions with peace activist Javier Sicilia on human rights issues and the government's security strategy. These discussions resulted in the creation of a Special Prosecutor for Victim Assistance (PROVICTIMA) in September, which assisted approximately 3,000 crime victims by year's end. Some NGOs, however, expressed frustration over the difficulty to engage in constructive human rights discussions with government officials.

The UN and NGOs reported harassment of human rights defenders. The CNDH received 59 complaints of aggression against human rights activists and 16 requests for protection. NGOs maintained that state and municipal authorities harassed defenders. The Inter-American Court of Human Rights ordered protective measures in six cases involving human rights defenders during the year. In July the president announced the launch of a national mechanism to protect human rights defenders.

Government Human Rights Bodies: The CNDH is the autonomous agency created by the government and funded by the legislature to monitor and act on human rights violations and abuses. It can call on government authorities to impose administrative sanctions or pursue criminal charges against officials, but it cannot impose legal sanctions itself. Whenever the relevant authority accepts a CNDH recommendation, the CNDH is required to follow up with the authority to ensure that it is, in fact, carrying out the recommendation. The CNDH sends a request to the authority asking for evidence of its compliance and reports this follow-up information in its annual report. When authorities fail to accept a recommendation, the CNDH makes that known publicly. NGOs and international organizations often drew attention to the failure of an institution to comply with or even accept CNDH recommendations. The CNDH was generally viewed by the public as unbiased and trustworthy. In June constitutional reforms increased the CNDH's capacity to investigate alleged violations and enforce its recommendations.

Each of the country's 31 states plus the Federal District has a state human rights commission autonomous from the CNDH.

Section 6. Discrimination, Societal Abuses, and Trafficking in Persons

The law prohibits discrimination based on race, gender, disability, language, or social status. While the government continued to make progress enforcing these provisions, significant problems, particularly violence against women, persisted.

Women

Rape and Domestic Violence: The law criminalizes rape, including spousal rape, and imposes penalties of up to 20 years' imprisonment. However, according to HRW and other NGOs, rape victims rarely filed complaints with police, in part because of the authorities' ineffective and unsupportive responses to victims, victims' fear of publicity, and a perception that prosecution of cases was unlikely. Human rights organizations asserted that authorities did not take seriously reports of rape, and victims continued to be socially stigmatized and ostracized.

Federal law prohibits domestic violence, including spousal abuse, and stipulates fines equal to 30 to 180 days' minimum salary and detention for up to 36 hours; actual sentences, however, were often more lenient. This countrywide law obligates federal and local authorities to prevent, punish, and eradicate violence against women. Nevertheless, according to the NGO Citizen Femicide Observatory (Observatorio Ciudadano de Feminicidios), domestic violence was pervasive and mostly unreported.

State-level laws sanctioning domestic violence are weak. Seven states do not criminalize it, and 15 states punish it only when it is a repeated offense. According to a survey conducted by the National Institute of Public Health in several of the country's rural and indigenous communities, victims did not report abuses for a variety of reasons, including fear of spousal reprisal, shame, and the view that the abuse did not merit a complaint. There were no authoritative statistics available on the number of abusers prosecuted, convicted, and punished. The 2006 National Survey on Household Relationships, the most recent such survey completed, suggested that 67 percent of women over age 15 had suffered some abusive treatment.

According to the Citizen Femicide Observatory, more than 1,700 girls, teenagers, and women were killed between January 2009 and June 2010.

The PGR's Special Prosecutor for Violence against Women and Trafficking in Persons (FEMVITRA) is responsible for leading government programs to combat domestic violence and federal human trafficking cases involving three or fewer suspects. With only five lawyers dedicated to federal cases of violence against women and trafficking countrywide as of 2010, FEMVITRA faced challenges in moving from investigations to convictions, although it achieved several.

There were approximately 70 government-funded shelters. Civil society and women's rights groups maintained numerous shelters as well.

Sexual Harassment: Federal law prohibits sexual harassment and provides for fines of up to 40 days' minimum salary. Sexual harassment is also criminalized in 26 states and the Federal District. Twenty-two of these states have provisions for punishment when the perpetrator is in a position of power. According to the National Women's Institute (INMUJERES), the federal government institution charged with directing national policy to achieve equality of opportunity between men and women, sexual harassment in the workplace was widespread, but victims were reluctant to come forward and cases were difficult to prove.

Sex Tourism: The country was a destination for sex tourists, particularly from the United States. There are no laws specifically prohibiting sex tourism with adults, although federal law criminalizes corruption of minors, for which the penalty is five to 10 years' imprisonment.

Reproductive Rights: Couples and individuals have the legal right to decide the number, spacing, and timing of children and have the information and means to do so free from discrimination. However, services, information, and public policies in the area of reproductive health were limited. Despite the existence of a national family planning program, the lack of sex education and contraceptives in public hospitals and rural areas undermined the government's commitment to reproductive rights. The Population Reference Bureau reported that 66 percent of women used modern contraceptives. Information on maternal health was available at public and private health clinics and online at the Federal Secretariat of Health's Web site. Skilled attendants at delivery and in postpartum care were widely available except in some marginalized areas. Women and men were given equal access to diagnostic services and treatment for sexually transmitted infections.

Discrimination: The law provides women the same rights and obligations as men and "equal pay ... for equal work performed in equal jobs, hours of work, and conditions of efficiency." According to INMUJERES, during the year women earned between 5 and 14 percent less than men for comparable work. INMUJERES reported that its national hotline received 5,881 calls during the year. The law provides labor protection for pregnant women. According to the Information Group on Reproductive Rights, some employers reportedly sought to avoid this law by requiring pregnancy tests in preemployment physicals and by continuing to make inquiries into a woman's reproductive status.

Children

Birth Registration: The country provides universal birth registration in principle, with citizenship derived both by birth within the country's territory and from one's parents.

Citizens generally registered the birth of newborns with local authorities. In some instances government officials visited private health institutions to facilitate the process. Failure to register births could result in the denial of public services, such as education or health care, to children living in communities where such services were in any event not widely available. According to UNICEF, 93.4 percent of children in the country were registered. However, states with large rural and indigenous populations, such as Chiapas, Guerrero, Oaxaca, and Puebla, had comparatively lower registration rates. According to UNICEF, as of 2009 only 61.7 percent of children in Chiapas were registered by their first birthday. At year's end, following appeals by UNICEF, the states of Oaxaca and Chiapas made birth registration free, resulting in the registration of thousands of previously unregistered children.

Child Abuse: In 2000--when the most recent survey was undertaken--the Federal Elections Institute and UNICEF reported that 28 percent of children ages six to nine, 9 percent of those ages 10 to 13, and 10 percent ages 14 to 17 reported being treated violently at home. According to the survey, 33 percent of rural children and youths and 26 percent of urban children and youths reported that adults sometimes resorted to insults and physical violence against children.

Child Marriage: Child marriage has historically been a problem, but no current statistics were available. The minimum marital age in the country is 14 for girls and 16 for boys with parental consent, and 18 without parental consent. UNICEF estimated that in 2008--the latest year for which information was available--approximately 19.2 percent of women and 4.5 percent of males married before the age of 18. Many of these marriages occurred in indigenous communities governed by the "usages and customs" regime.

Sexual Exploitation of Children: The antitrafficking law prohibits the commercial sexual exploitation of children. UNICEF reported that approximately 16,000 children were involved in commercial sexual exploitation. It was not uncommon to find minors engaged in prostitution. The NGOs Center for Studies and Investigation in Development and Social Assistance, Casa Alianza, and National Network of Shelters reported that sex tourism and sexual exploitation of minors were significant problems in resort towns and northern border areas.

The country does not have a statutory rape law, but it has laws against corruption of a minor and child pornography that apply to victims under 18 years of age. For the crimes of selling, distributing, or promoting pornography to a minor, the law stipulates a prison term of six months to five years and a fine of 300 to 500 times the daily minimum wage. For the crime of involving minors in acts of sexual exhibitionism, the law mandates seven to 12 years in prison and a fine of 800 to 2,500 times the daily minimum wage. The production, facilitation, reproduction, distribution, sale, and purchase of child pornography carries a punishment of seven to 12 years' in prison and a fine of 800 to 2,000 times the daily minimum wage.

Perpetrators who promote, publicize, or facilitate sexual tourism involving minors, face seven to 12 years' imprisonment and a fine of 800 to 2,000 times the daily minimum wage. For those involved in sexual tourism who commit a sexual act with a minor, the law requires a 12- to 18-year prison sentence and a fine of 2,000 to 3,000 times the daily minimum wage. The crime of sexual exploitation of a minor carries an eight- to 15-year prison sentence and a fine of 1,000 to 2,500 times the daily minimum wage.

Institutionalized Children: The NGO Disability Rights International found in a 2010 study that mentally disabled children in orphanages and care facilities were subject to a number of grave abuses, including trafficking in persons (see Persons with Disabilities below).

International Child Abductions: The country is a party to the 1980 Hague Convention on the Civil Aspects of International Child Abduction. For information see the Department of State's report on compliance at http://travel.state.gov/abduction/resources/congressreport/congressreport_4308.html as well as country-specific information at http://travel.state.gov/abduction/country/country_3781.html.

Anti-Semitism

There were no reports of anti-Semitic acts. According to the 2010 census, the Jewish community numbered approximately 67,000 persons.

Trafficking in Persons

See the Department of State's *Trafficking in Persons Report* at www.state.gov/j/tip.

Persons with Disabilities

The law prohibits discrimination against persons with physical, sensory, intellectual, and mental disabilities in employment, education, access to health care, and the provision of other services. However, the government did not effectively enforce all these stipulations. Public buildings and facilities in Mexico City did not comply with the law requiring access for persons with disabilities, although the federal government stated that entrances, exits, and hallways in all of its offices were accessible to persons with disabilities. The education system provided special education for approximately 485,170 students with disabilities nationwide.

According to the National Commission for Persons with Disabilities, 63 percent of children with disabilities between the ages of six and 14 attended school, compared with 92 percent for those in the same age range without disabilities. Only 4 percent of the overall population with disabilities had finished university. According to the National Council to Prevent Discrimination, 60 percent of all persons with disabilities reported insufficient access to public or private health care. The CNDH received 41 complaints of discrimination against persons with physical disabilities and six complaints of discrimination against persons with mental disabilities during the year.

The secretary of health collaborated with the secretaries of social development, labor, and public education, as well as with the Integral Development of the Family (DIF) and the Office for the Promotion and Social Integration of the Disabled, to protect the rights of persons with disabilities. The government established offices and programs for the social integration of persons with disabilities, including a program to enhance job opportunities and launch an online portal to disseminate information and assistance.

In its 2010 study, Disability Rights International (DRI) found widespread human rights abuses in mental institutions and care facilities across the country, including those for children. Abuses against disabled persons included lack of access to justice, the use of physical and chemical restraints and unconsented lobotomies on some patients, physical and sexual abuse, and trafficking of children with mental disabilities. Persons with disabilities often lacked adequate privacy and clothing and often ate, slept, and bathed in unhygienic conditions. They were vulnerable to abuse from staff members, other patients, or outsiders at facilities where there was little supervision.

DRI reported in 2010 that at the Samuel Ramirez Moreno Psychiatric Hospital in Mexico City, a man was restrained with a helmet and arm restraints during the day and bed restraints at night from at least March to September 2010. Authorities at the institution stated that long-term restraints were the only option they had to control the patient and that they were not administering any other form of treatment or therapy to improve his condition.

At the Cruz del Sur Psychiatric Hospital in Oaxaca in 2010, DRI investigators found a woman being held in a bed with restraints despite evidenced distress because she spoke an indigenous language that no member of the staff knew. The staff planned to keep her in restraints until members of her family arrived and could translate.

According to a 2010 survey by the National Council to Prevent Discrimination, 55 percent of persons with disabilities reported an income insufficient to cover their basic needs. More than 50 percent of those surveyed stated that their primary source of income was their family and only 40 percent reported having a job.

Indigenous People

The CNDH and the State Secretariat of Indigenous Peoples in Chiapas acknowledged that indigenous communities have long been socially and economically marginalized and subjected to discrimination, particularly in the central and southern regions, where indigenous persons sometimes represented more than one-third of the total state population. In the state of Chiapas, the NGOs Fray Bartolome de las Casas and International Service for Peace argued that indigenous peoples' ability to participate in decisions affecting their lands, cultural traditions, and allocation of natural resources was negligible.

Indigenous groups claimed that the country's legal framework neither respected, nor prevented violations of, the property rights of indigenous communities. Communities and NGOs representing indigenous groups reported that the government did not consult indigenous communities adequately when making decisions about development project implementation on indigenous land. There was also limited consultation with indigenous communities regarding the exploitation of energy, minerals, timber, and other natural resources on indigenous lands.

Indigenous persons did not live on autonomous reservations, although some indigenous communities exercised considerable local control over economic, political, and social matters. In Oaxaca State, for example, 70 percent of the 570 municipalities were governed according to the indigenous regime of "usages and customs," which did not follow democratic norms such as the secret ballot, universal suffrage, and political affiliation.

In May authorities detained Rufino Juarez Hernandez, the head of the Union of Social Well-Being of the Triqui Region, in connection with the April 2010 killings of two members of a humanitarian aid mission traveling in Oaxaca. Members of the European Parliament, who visited the country in September to determine the status of the case, applauded the detention but noted the justice system's continued failure to bring the crime to trial.

The government generally showed respect for the desire of indigenous persons to retain elements of their traditional culture. The law provides for educational instruction in the national language, Spanish, without prejudice to the protection and promotion of indigenous languages. However, many indigenous children spoke only their native languages. In practice education in indigenous languages was limited by the lack of textbooks and teaching materials, as well as by the lack of qualified teachers fluent in these languages.

During the year the CNDH received 27 complaints and issued two recommendations on human rights abuses of the indigenous population. Most complaints pertained to a lack of interpreters and discriminatory practices by government officials.

NGOs such as Fray Bartolome de las Casas and International Service for Peace reported that state authorities and nongovernmental actors harassed and abused indigenous human rights defenders.

In June the Tlachinollan Mountain Human Rights Center in Ayutla de los Libres, Guerrero, which reopened that month, reported security threats, including instances of soldiers entering employees' homes without a warrant (see section 1.f.).

In October 2010 the Inter-American Court of Human Rights ruled on the cases of Organization of the Me'phaa Indigenous People members Valentina Rosendo Cantu and Ines Fernandez Ortega, indigenous women whom soldiers detained arbitrarily and raped in separate incidents in 2002. The court ordered the military to compensate the victims and their families, who had complained of harassment and intimidation by soldiers in the area since the court accepted the cases in 2006. In August the military declined jurisdiction over the cases and the PGR accepted jurisdiction. The federal government held a public ceremony in December in honor of the victims, complying with one aspect of the Inter-American Court ruling. The cases remained pending in federal courts at year's end.

The OHCHR, as well as NGOs AI, International Service for Peace, and the Network of All Rights for All, reported that Chiapas-based human rights defender Margarita Martinez and staff members of NGO Fray Bartolome de las Casas received death threats in November 2010 and October 2011 in connection with their work on human rights for indigenous groups in Chiapas. The group continued to receive protection, including from police, as instructed by the IACHR.

Societal Abuses, Discrimination, and Acts of Violence Based on Sexual Orientation and Gender Identity

While Mexican society increasingly accepted the lesbian, gay, bisexual, and transgender (LGBT) communities, the CNDH and the National Center to Prevent and Control HIV/AIDS stated that discrimination based on sexual orientation and gender identity persisted. In separate incidents during the year, unknown assailants killed two prominent LGBT activists. Authorities in both instances stated that the killings were "crimes of passion" within the gay community. Activists noted that this characterization was misleading and oversimplified patterns of violence against LGBT persons.

On May 3, Guerrero-based LGBT activist Quetzalcoatl Leija Herrera was found beaten to death near the city of Chilpancingo's central plaza.

On July 23, security guards discovered the body of Cristian Ivan Sanchez Venancio in his home near the center of Mexico City. Sanchez, a member of the Revolutionary Democratic Party's Coordinating Group for Sexual Diversity and an organizer of Mexico City's annual LGBT Pride Parade, was stabbed to death.

Other Societal Violence or Discrimination

There were no reports of societal violence or discrimination against persons with HIV/AIDS.

The CNDH alleged in August that the PGR was withholding information on a case in Tamaulipas in which 72 migrants were kidnapped from a bus and killed, reportedly by TCO members, in August 2010. The CNDH claimed the PGR's delay prevented them from making a recommendation. Another 50 migrants were reportedly kidnapped in Oaxaca in December 2010 by unknown persons. While one individual was arrested in June in connection with the Tamaulipas case, both cases remained under investigation at year's end. These and other high-profile crimes against migrants prompted the passage in May of a comprehensive migration law intended to protect the human rights of migrants. At year's end the government continued working with civil society groups to define the implementing regulations for the law.

The INM operated 52 migrant detention centers. The CNDH had an office in each of these facilities to monitor compliance for respect of detainee human rights. During its April visit, however, the UN Committee on the Protection of the Rights of All Migrant Workers and Members of their Families expressed concern over the conditions and treatment of migrants at the centers and recommended improving facilities and investigating allegations of abuse by authorities.

There were no developments in the September 2010 deaths of two suspected kidnappers in Asencion, Chihuahua, at the hands of a vigilante mob.

Section 7. Worker Rights

a. Freedom of Association and the Right to Collective Bargaining

Federal law provides workers the right to form and join unions, provides for the right to strike in both the public and private sector, and protects the right to bargain collectively. However, the law places several restrictions on these rights. The law does not prohibit antiunion discrimination nor require reinstatement of workers fired for union activity.

Although the law requires a minimum of only 20 workers to form an independent union, it requires official recognition from the government to register the union formally and establishes administrative procedures for registration. The law prohibits the coexistence of two or more unions in the same state agency. Article 372 of the labor law bans foreign nationals from being members of trade union executive bodies. It also includes an "exclusion clause," which allows employers to terminate the contract of an employee who quits the union. During the year the Supreme Court of Justice determined that the exclusion clause was unconstitutional, however, the law had not been modified by year's end.

A union that has been established in accordance with its own bylaws may call for a strike or bargain collectively. The government can grant legal recognition to unions, a process known as "toma de nota," either to union executive leaders individually or to the entire executive committee. The law also limits the right to strike of a number of public officials, including many that do not exercise authority in the name of the government, restricts government employees--including banking sector employees--from striking unless there is a "systematic violation of their rights", and requires that a two-thirds majority of workers in the relevant public service entity must be in favor of a strike. Before a strike may be considered legal, a union must file a "notice to strike" with the appropriate labor authorities.

Although the law authorizes the coexistence of several unions, it sets rules on which union has priority and limits collective bargaining to the union that has the largest number of workers. Migrant workers are excluded from relevant legal protections.

The government did not consistently protect these rights in practice. Its general failure to enforce labor and other laws left workers without much recourse with regard to violations of freedom of association, working conditions, or other problems. Union organizers from several sectors complained about the overt and usually hostile involvement of the government when organizers attempted to develop independent unions. The process for official government recognition of unions was politicized, and the government occasionally used the process to reward political allies or punish political opponents. According to union organizers, government labor boards frequently rejected union registration applications on technicalities. In addition, independent union activists claimed that the requirement that the government approve strikes in advance gave authorities the power to show favoritism by determining which companies would be protected from strikes.

Although few formal strikes occurred, in part because of the numerous restrictions on strikes, informal stoppages of work by both union and nonunionized groups were fairly common. According to union activists, employers frequently did not attend conciliation meetings between the parties as a stalling tactic.

Protection (company-controlled) unions continued to be a problem in all sectors, and many observers noted that a majority of organized workers belonged to unrepresentative unions. Officially sanctioned "protection contracts"--formal agreements whereby the company created an unrepresentative union in exchange for labor peace and other concessions--were common in all sectors and often prevented workers from fully exercising their labor rights as defined by law. These contracts were often developed prior to the company hiring any workers at a new job site and managed without direct input from workers. Collective bargaining agreements resulting from protection contracts usually failed to provide worker benefits beyond the legal minimum and impeded the rights of independent unions to effectively and legitimately bargain collectively on behalf of workers.

According to several NGOs and unions, many workers continued to face intimidation during bargaining rights elections from other workers, union leaders, or employers favoring a particular union. The practice of a voice vote was declared illegal by the Supreme Court. However, practices such as providing very limited notice prior to an election and allowing management or nonemployees to vote were increasingly common.

An October 31 election at the Telefonica-affiliated Atento Services was cancelled due to reports of violence. Workers at the call center were reportedly subjected to violence and intimidation by thugs outside the voting place and prohibited from entering. Workers claimed that they had planned to try to elect a nonprotection union, Telefonistas de la Republica Mexicana. The vote was subsequently rescheduled for November 9, and a protection union won. Workers sympathetic to Telefonistas de la Republica Mexicana claimed that they were again prohibited from voting.

Workers were reportedly expelled from official unions for trying to organize their colleagues into separate, independent unions. The "exclusion clause" in law gave these unions the right to prevent the formation of an authentic union by expelling agitators from the "official" union, thereby obliging the company to fire these individuals. Some fired workers accused unions of harassment and intimidation.

At the end of 2010, the offices of the Worker Support Center (Centro de Apoyo al Trabajador - CAT) were looted and threatening messages were targeted at employees in response to the CAT's efforts to support workers at the Johnson Controls Interiors plant in Puebla. The leader of CAT received death threats. By April the Johnson Controls Interiors workers had ousted the "protection union" and signed a new agreement that included a 7.5 percent wage increase and better working conditions. However, CAT and its director continued to receive threats during the year, and its offices were again robbed. Authorities subsequently responded to the threats by instituting routine police patrols by CAT offices and providing dedicated cell phones to the CAT leadership in case of an emergency. The investigation continued at year's end.

b. Prohibition of Forced or Compulsory Labor

Although the law prohibits all forms of forced or compulsory labor, the government did not effectively enforce such laws. Forced labor persisted in both the agricultural and industrial sectors. Women and children were subjected to domestic servitude. Migrants, including men, women, and children, were the most vulnerable to forced labor.

Also see the Department of State's *Trafficking in Persons Report* at www.state.gov/j/tip.

c. Prohibition of Child Labor and Minimum Age for Employment

The law prohibits children under the age of 14 from working and allows those between the ages of 14 and 17 to work limited daytime hours in nonhazardous conditions, and only with parental permission.

The government did not effectively enforce such prohibitions. According to sources including the International Labor Organization, government enforcement was reasonably effective at large and medium-sized companies, especially in factories run by U.S. companies, or the "maquila" sector, and other industries under federal jurisdiction; inadequate at many small companies and in the agriculture and construction sectors, and nearly absent in the informal sector, in which most children worked. The labor inspection process is complicated by complex divisions and a lack of coordination between federal and state jurisdictions. The Secretariat for Social Development, the PGR, and the National System for Integral Family Development all have responsibility for enforcement of some aspects of child labor laws or intervention in cases where such laws are violated. The Secretariat of Labor and Social Security (STPS) is responsible for carrying out child labor inspections.

The STPS was involved in programs that supported the elimination of child labor and the improvement of conditions for legally working minors. Beginning in September the STPS implemented a campaign in Baja California to educate workers and employers about agriculture workers' rights in 26 states. The STPS continued to work with global donors to implement programs to combat child labor in the agriculture sector, including in Michoacan, Veracruz, Chiapas, and Sinaloa. During the year the Secretariat for Social Development and DIF carried out programs to prevent child labor abuses and promote child labor rights, including specific efforts to combat the commercial sexual exploitation of children.

Child labor remained a problem. According to the most current government child labor survey, conducted between 2007 and 2009 by the National Institute of Statistics and Geography and the Ministry of Labor, the overall child occupation rate (five to 17 years old) fell from 12.5 percent to 10.7 percent, or approximately 3 million children. Forty-two percent of child labor occurred in the livestock and the agricultural sectors. Child labor in agriculture included the production of melons, onions, sugarcane, tobacco, and tomatoes. Other sectors with significant child labor included commerce, services, manufacturing, and construction.

d. Acceptable Conditions of Work

The minimum daily wage, determined by zone, was 59.82 pesos ($4.29) in Zone A (Baja California, Federal District, state of Mexico, and large cities), 58.13 pesos ($4.16) in Zone B (Sonora, Nuevo Leon, Tamaulipas, Veracruz, and Jalisco), and 56.70 pesos ($4.06) in Zone C (all other states). Most formal sector workers received between one and three times the minimum wage. The National Council for Evaluation of Social Development Policy estimated the poverty line at 64 pesos ($4.58) per day for 2011.

The law sets six eight-hour days and 48 hours per week as the legal workweek. Any work more than eight hours in a day is considered overtime, for which a worker receives double the hourly wage. After accumulating nine hours of overtime in a week, a worker earns triple the hourly wage, the law prohibits compulsory overtime. The law includes eight paid public holidays, and one week of paid annual leave after completing one year of work. The law requires employers to observe occupational safety and health regulations, issued jointly by the STPS and the Mexican Institute for Social Security. Legally mandated joint management and labor committees set standards and are responsible for overseeing workplace standards in plants and offices. Individual employees or unions may complain directly to inspectors or safety and health officials. By law workers may remove themselves from hazardous situations without jeopardizing their employment.

The STPS is responsible for enforcing labor laws and employed 376 federal labor inspectors during the year, compared with 218 in 2007. The STPS carried out regular inspections of workplaces, using a questionnaire to identify victims of labor exploitation. Between January and November, it undertook 56,390 inspections, including the monitoring of industries identified as having a high incidence of child labor (agriculture, coal mines, and construction work). These operations identified 1,836 underage agricultural workers, removed workers under age 14, and penalized employers with fines. According to the STPS, training for labor inspectors included a program focused on enforcement of labor laws in the agricultural sector, but there was no program for labor inspections in the informal sector.

In practice workers often could not remove themselves from hazardous situations without jeopardizing their employment. According to labor rights NGOs, employers in all sectors sometimes used the illegal "hours bank" approach--requiring long hours when the workload is heavy and cutting hours when it is light--to avoid compensating workers for overtime. In addition many companies evaded taxes and social security payments by employing workers informally. The Organization for Economic Cooperation and Development estimated that 43 percent of the workforce was engaged in the informal economy.

Environmental groups criticized the hazardous working conditions in mines, including exposure to methane gas and mercury poisoning. For instance, 14 workers were killed in a methane explosion on May 3, and on August 26, four workers were killed while working in a coal mine in Coahuila. The union blamed the incidents on a lack of sufficient safety controls.

ABOUT THE AUTHOR

Brian D. Lerner is an Immigration Lawyer and runs a National Immigration Law Firm for nearly 30 years. He is an attorney who is a certified specialist that might help in Immigration & Nationality Law as issued by the California State Bar, Board of Legal Specialization. Attorney Lerner is an expert in Immigration Law, Removal and Deportation, Citizenship, Waiver and Appeals.

He has been a licensed attorney since 1992 and started the Law Offices of Brian D. Lerner, APC. The immigration practice consists of Immigration and Nationality Law, and everything involved with and regarding immigration which includes citizenship, investment visas, family and employment visas, removal and deportation hearings, appeals, waivers, adjustment, consulate processing and all types of immigration and citizenship matters.

He has represented clients from all over the U.S. and in many countries around the world. One side of his practice is dedicated to keeping people in the U.S. and fighting for their immigration rights, while another side is to get people back who have been deported and removed from the U.S.

Also, there is the affirmative part of Immigration Law which Brian Lerner has helped numerous people come into the U.S. on business visas, investment visas, student visas, fiancée and marriage visas, religious visas and many more. Attorney Lerner has helped immigrants who are victims of crime and domestic violence or ones that are married to abusers.

In other words, Attorney Lerner has a firm that helps people all over the U.S. He has dedicated significant time to preparing numerous petitions and applications for you to get at a fraction of the price of hiring an attorney. He says it is the next best thing to a real attorney because they are real petitions prepared by an expert.

www.ingramcontent.com/pod-product-compliance
Lightning Source LLC
Chambersburg PA
CBHW051800200326
41597CB00025B/4637

9 781958 990087